FREEDOM TODAY

THEOLOGICAL MEDITATIONS, edited by Hans Küng

Forthcoming Titles:

The God of Every Day
Gotthold Hasenhüttl, "The Unknown God"
Herbert Haag, "The God of the Beginnings . . . and of Today"
Karl Rahner, "God in Daily Things"

Spirit and Life
Karl Hermann Schelkle, "A Priestly People"
Michael Pfliegler, "Celibacy"
Karl Rahner, "To Believe Today"

THEOLOGICAL MEDITATIONS ·

Freedom Today

by HANS KÜNG

translated by Cecily Hastings

SHEED AND WARD · NEW YORK

Library of Congress Catalog Card Number 65–20861

Nihil obstat:
   Thomas J. Beary
   Censor Librorum

Imprimatur:
   Patrick C. Brennan
   Vicar General
   Diocese of Burlington
   December 7, 1965

Manufactured in the United States of America

Gratefully Dedicated to
Boston College and
St. Louis University

Introduction to the Series
"Theological Meditations"

Theologians complain that our devotional literature has long been, and still is, overly superficial and moralistic, that it all too rarely stems from the center of the Christian message, that it commonly lacks true orientation to biblical perspectives, that it does not give adequate recognition to the important advances theology has made on so many fronts in our age. In short, they object that our devotional writing is gravely lacking in "theological" substance.

Non-theologians also take issue with theologians in this dispute. They complain that our theological literature likewise has long been, and continues to be, by and large esoteric and intellectualistic, that it frequently disdains to rub shoulders with the real world, indeed that it rarely, if ever, displays real concern for the needs of people living today, that it fails to speak the language of our time, and that it almost never makes a clear and decisive call to the imitation of Christ. In short, they object that our theological writing generally fails to "edify" in the best and most important sense of the word.

Such complaints are hardly new. Essentially they date back to the period when, with theology becoming institutionalized and with Aristotelianism beginning to cast its shadow across the intellectual world, the oneness of scientific and devotional theology, the unity between dogma and spirituality, could no longer stand intact. What early Church theology with Origen and Athanasius, Augustine and Jerome, the two Cyrils and the Cappadocian represented as a perfectly self-evident and natural unit, what the Areopagite, Maximos and John Damascene and then Anselm and Bernard all carried on, what Albert the Great, Bonaventure and Thomas Aquinas were able, not without enormous straining to be sure, to hold together, fell neatly apart in the age that succeeded them. The thinker and the man of piety, the dogmatist and the mystic, the theologian and the saint were each to go his separate way.

Yet so much of the upheaval witnessed in the theology, in the Church, and in the world of our century compels us to try to re-see and re-practice as one single theology the separate disciplines of scientific and devotional theology. In the final analysis, a Christian cannot but consider learning and piety, study and devotion, and indeed theology and meditation as belonging essentially together. Theological research carried on without reverence and meditation easily degenerates into a speculating or historicizing scholasticism that lacks life. Similarly, pious meditation engaged in without the sobering restraints of clear theological norms has a way of degenerating into an intellectually inbred or sentimental religiosity that lacks substance.

But this is no easy task, particularly in an age when exegesis and dogmatic theology have been subjected to the methods of history-criticism. And the theologian is certainly overburdened if he is expected to work both scientifically and devotionally in everything he does. For we must never forget that theology is basically quite different from preaching, that it is not simply the proclamation of the Good News. Theology admittedly must serve preaching and the proclamation of the Gospel—but it is precisely those tools acquired by scholarly research that theology must use in this service. And it is in rendering this specific service to preaching and to the propagation of the Good News that theology will succeed in attaining its ultimate aim and purpose.

The volumes of our series are not intended as substitutes for that to which the theologian must always direct and orient whatever he does. But it is hoped that they will do expressly and directly that which the theologian all too often, in his dedication to extracting from things what is essential to theology, must do only indirectly and by implication. We hope to tie theology and meditation together in various important ways, and to practice the two as a single activity. Thus we shall strive not only to think out and to examine problems according to the strict disciplines of research, but also to ponder reflectively over God's Word, considering what that Word, be it familiar or foreign to us, truly signifies for us today, here and now. It is a *meditari*, a pondering and reflecting which is not a form of contemplation that would be an end in itself, but which will rather tend, come what may of opposition, almost of itself to lead us to prayer and works. The progression must begin with theological *meditatio*, then pass through *tentatio* to *oratio* and *actio* in the imitation of Christ. This theological meditation will vary with the theologian who is executing it, be he Old Testament scholar, New Testament scholar, or systematic theologian. But the source from which it draws will always be the same, namely God's Word, and the end to which it tends will always be the same, namely man here and now. That said, the following words of St. John will always apply: "Let us show our love by the true test of action, not by taking phrases on our lips" (1 John 3, 18).

Preface

The times are long past when we paged through specifically
Catholic theological dictionaries in vain for the heading "Freedom," or, if not totally in vain, we found ourselves directed
to the heading "Law." Not only in Christianity in general, but
within the Catholic Church as well, it is now perfectly clear
that "freedom" is not, and must not become, a scarce com-
modity or a luxury reserved to special groups. Freedom is the
right, indeed it is the very grace, of each and every Christian
person. Freedom is God's supreme gift to men. Freedom is
the sacred duty of men who will live in the service of God.

This book is an attempt to examine what all this means for
us today:

What it means for the *individual Christian* in the world—
we are reminded of Thomas More—what it means to live in
the world freely according to the Gospel.

What it means for the *Church*: Just what is the true freedom of the Church as she finds herself in the world and how
should she realize this freedom for herself?

What it means for *theology*: Just how free and especially

to what end must the free Church's theology, upon which the Church's freedom to such a great extent depends, be free?

What it means for *religions:* How can the Church show her freedom to the world religions and what can she give them by way of freedom?

What it means for a *Pope*—the unforgettable John XXIII—to what extent did he realize, in an exemplary manner, the freedom of a Christian person?

The individual themes overlap frequently. For example, how can there be freedom for the individual without freedom for the Church, and vice versa, or how can the Church be free without theology being free, and vice versa? If Christian freedom is to be all-embracing and is to pervade every aspect of life, it must be enlightened and viewed from different angles. Thus we shall change our emphasis according to the particular themes of the various parts of this book. For example, in the first and the last chapters, we find we must speak more personally since we are considering concrete models of Christian freedom such as Thomas More and John XXIII; or more objectively in other chapters where an objective presentation of the problem area is called for and does not permit much departure from a sober theological examination.

Shall I pass over how sincerely I rejoice that this book is to appear in its present form for the first time in the United States of America? The history of the United States is in a most unique and significant way bound to the very stuff of freedom. Furthermore, for me personally, the subject "freedom" is tied indissolubly to the United States and to the Church in the United States. For it was there that I spoke for the first time on the Church and Freedom, and it was there that I experienced for the first time how much joy, how much hope and energy emanates from the very word "freedom." I shall never be able to give adequate expression to the gratitude I feel for all that this experience has meant to me.

To Boston College, then, the university which first extended its invitation for me to come to America, and to St. Louis University, to which I am indebted for an honorary degree of Doctor of Laws, this book is sincerely and gratefully dedicated.

HANS KÜNG

Tübingen, December 1965

Contents

Contents

I THE FREEDOM OF THE INDIVIDUAL

You were called to freedom!
Gal. 5, 13

Free—from what?
I should see it shining in your eyes: Free—for what?
Friedrich Nietzsche

A Saint in the World?

Looking at the famous painting of Thomas More by Holbein, we often ask ourselves: Is this the face of a "saint"? It is indeed a wonderful face: the eyes are serenely thoughtful, critical, you might almost say sceptical, yet not hard, but kindly; the nose and mouth indicate discipline and moderation, unforced assurance and firmness; the whole is of a simple, natural cast, making it a likable face. A fine, strong face; but a saint's face?

We can almost read the man's past history from the face: student at Oxford at fourteen, and afterwards in London; at twenty-two, the friend of Erasmus of Rotterdam and himself a brilliant humanist and jurist; at twenty-six, Member of Parliament; then Under-Sheriff of the City of London and Reader in Law at Lincoln's Inn; diplomat and ambassador at thirty-seven; Under-Treasurer of England at forty-three; then Speaker of the Lower House, and High Steward of the Universities of Oxford and Cambridge; finally, at fifty-one, Lord Chancellor and first statesman of the realm. Such was Sir Thomas More, whose picture ("immeasurably more beautiful than any reproduction of it") Hans Holbein has given us. But once again: Is this the picture of a saint?*

This is not an idle question for the Christian who is trying to live by the Gospel in the world. Because it is not posed abstractly and theoretically, but attached to a concrete, existing human being, it can be made an extremely pressing question on one's own Christian existence in the world. Only too often the Christian comes up against the question whether it is possible at all to live as a Christian in the world; meaning, not just to get along somehow, but to live by the Gospel. Rather, if one really wants to live by the Gospel, does one not have to forsake the world and retire into the desert or into a monastery? Thomas More lived in the world; indeed, he was "a man of the world." Urbane, self-assured, distinguished, with perfect manners (learned in boyhood in the household of Lord Chancellor Morton), this great scholar, diplomat and orator had a command not only of Latin but also—a matter of hard labor to the early humanists—of Greek, and was at the same time a supreme master of English prose. He was personally acquainted with the greatest scholars not only of England (Colet, Grocyn, Linacre) but of all Europe, and conducted an extensive correspondence: with the Spaniard Vives, the Frenchman Budé, the Dutch Erasmus; Holbein was for a long while his guest. His history of Richard III, which had a profound influence on Shakespeare, was the start of English historical writing. His *Utopia*, the first of a whole series of "ideal states," is, with Machiavelli's *Prince*, which

* The data on Thomas More's life are taken from the admirable biography *Thomas More*, by R. W. Chambers (Westminster, Md., Newman, 1949). See also *The Correspondence of Sir Thomas More*, ed. Elizabeth Frances Rogers (Princeton, 1947).

appeared in the same year, the most influential book on the State produced in the sixteenth century. Yet this man of the world with his towering intelligence, his iron resolution, his high sense of justice and his fearless bearing (of which he had given evidence as a young man in Parliament, when, regardless of danger, he spoke in a financial debate against the miserly Henry VII), was at the same time possessed of an enchanting modesty, friendliness and amiability. *Gravitas* with both *suavitas* and *festivitas* were his characteristics, according to the witness of contemporaries. Deep seriousness was coupled in this "man for all seasons" with a humor that became proverbial. Even in his boyhood as a page he had been an excellent actor (and wrote little plays himself); he was one of the greatest masters of irony, so that Erasmus, punning on his name, dedicated to him that one of his works which is most popular in character, the *Moriae Encomium*, or *Praise of Folly*. More had the trick of producing his jests with so solemn a countenance that even his own family was constantly taken in by them; jest and earnest were never easy to distinguish in him.

Is it any wonder that Sir Thomas More was admired throughout Europe and that there were those in England who consciously imitated him? There was a man "who, being most unlike unto him in wit and learning, nevertheless in wearing his gown awry upon the one shoulder, as Sir Thomas More was wont to do, would needs be counted like unto him." "Thomas More, Lord Chancellor of England, whose soul was more pure than any snow, whose genius was such as England never had—yea, and never shall have again, mother of good wits though England be. . . ." So wrote Erasmus on receiving the news of More's death. Thomas More; great genius, great humanist. Thomas More—a great "saint" as well? The Gospel demands more than pure, noble *humanitas*; the following of Christ more than creative genius.

Property, Family, State

When we look at this man, does it seem as though the Sermon on the Mount had counted for anything with him? This is the question which we here focus on Thomas More, but whose application is to us, who are Christians in the world. It can be made more explicit by reference to the evangelical "counsels" (often misunderstood in the sense of a two-level morality) of poverty, celibacy and obedience. It is true that this listing together of the three evangelical counsels represents a later theological systematization. But the first two have their basis directly in the New Testament. And even though it is not possible in principle to measure all Christian existence by them and them alone, yet when properly, i.e., scripturally, understood they can face the Christian in the world with an acutely critical question.

There is no escaping the impression that Thomas More was committed in exactly the opposite direction. Christian sociologists often give the three pillars of the social order as the family, property, and the State. They explain them like this: The task that God has given man is the individual working out of the fulfillment of his own person within his human nature. First, the fulfillment of the human person, as it were, inwards; the community of marriage, through mutual, loving self-giving and the support and upbringing of the children. Hence the social institution and function of the *family*, because this is the only way of guaranteeing a sensible ordering of things in this sphere. At the same time, the human person must be fulfilled in an outward direction; by addressing himself to the world of material things without which man's life is impossible. Hence the social institution and function of *private property*, as the one way in which material goods can give the free human personality its full development and value, the one way of taking care of the future for the individual and his family, and finally the one way of preserving and advancing the common good, social order and social peace. But because family relationships and economic relationships are, independently of each other, in a constant state of change, and because these two spheres of life exist in relation to each other in a state of dialectical tension and development, there has to be regulation by law, and there has to be a power which gives that law permanence. Hence the social institution and function of the *State*, which—not as the only guarantee of the rule of law, yet as its highest guarantee—has the task of coordinating the rights and duties of individuals and providing them with a permanent structure, so that the human person may thus pursue its full and lasting integration in security and peace.

Thus speak the sociologists. The family, private property, and the State as guaranteeing the rule of law, are according to them necessary to the fulfillment of man's task in life, to man's realization of himself as a person. Precisely in this way —because man can only exist as a social being—they are necessary for the ordering of the whole life of the community, at the family, social and political levels. Family, property and State appear as the three pillars of order in the life of society.

But is it not strange to see how, to the scandal of sociologists, these very pillars of order are, for the Christian setting out to follow Christ, called in question by the Gospel? If we look at the three props and stays of order and the three evangelical "counsels," is it not striking how precisely they correspond to each other, or rather contradict each other? Christian perfection is to consist in poverty, celibacy and obedience. Does not freely chosen poverty contradict property, freely chosen celibacy, the family, and freely chosen obedience, as a renunciation of rights and power, that binding rule of law which the State is there to guarantee?

But Thomas More seems to have stood very firmly indeed by these three principal pillars of the secular social order.

Property: Sir Thomas had an extremely fine house in London, on the banks of the Thames at Chelsea, with a library, a gallery, a chapel, a park and orchard. He maintained a numerous household, and his house was full of curious and remarkable things; anything that came from abroad or was otherwise of great interest he would buy immediately, and it gave him pleasure when other people took delight in these things. He took particular pleasure in studying the forms and characteristics of animals. He kept a whole menagerie, with innumerable species of birds and other rare animals: beavers, weasels, foxes. . . . His great favorite was his monkey, immortalized as part of the More family portrait and praised for its cleverness by Erasmus, who had watched it engaged in a game with a weasel. Thus Thomas More, who took particular pleasure in fools and himself maintained a fool as part of his household, lived a happy life in the midst of his family and his numerous friends and visitors, "with no aversion from innocent pleasure."

Family: At the age of twenty-seven or twenty-eight Sir Thomas married the seventeen-year-old Jane Colt, whom he dearly loved and tried to educate. She bore him three daughters, Margaret, Cecily and Elizabeth, and one son, John. After the early death of his wife he married a second time; Dame Alice, elderly and not very amiable, was at least a good housewife. He was greatly attached to his children. He gave his daughters the same humanist education as his son, well aware of this as a bold innovation which would bring him criticism. Margaret, in particular, attained a noteworthy degree of learning, with much-admired Latinity. More thought of his children throughout all the demands made on him by his activity as a statesman, even when on embassies or journeying in attendance on the King. He expected a letter from each of them every day. He answered them in Latin prose or Latin verses, and wrote these even when riding, soaked through with rain, on a horse stumbling or stuck in the mud. He loved to remember how he had given them fine silk clothes and fed them with cakes and fruit, and beaten them, when strictly necessary, only with peacocks' feathers. Is it any wonder that More's foster-daughter, Margaret Gigs, used to commit small faults simply for the pleasure of being scolded and noticed by More?

The State: Sir Thomas More's whole life was devoted to the State and the defense of the rule of law. In his native city of London, his name became a legend above all for his work as a judge. Never before or after in England had every man come by his own so well and so swiftly. "Howbeit, this one thing, son," said More to one of his sons-in-law, "I assure thee on my faith, that if the parties will at my hands call for justice, then, all were it my father stood on the one side, and the Devil on the other, his cause being good, the Devil should have right." There are many anecdotes illustrating More's display of the wisdom of Solomon. Under More's predecessor as Chancellor, Wolsey, business had piled up enormously. When More took office, there were cases outstanding that had been introduced twenty years before. His profound knowledge of the law and his astonishing gift of quick comprehension brought him to that day of triumph when he took his seat, settled a case, called for the next one—and there were no more to come. He had the fact recorded in the public acts of the Court. Along with his humor, it was this above all that made him a legend. Decades later, the epigrams were praising him:

> When More some time had Chancellor been,
>   No more suits did remain.
> The like will never more be seen
>   Till More be there again.

More carried out all his State business with the same combination of deliberation and devotion. Unlike Erasmus, who was at home nowhere and everywhere, he was filled with a genuinely English, and at the same time European, patriotism, which even led him into a quarrel with a French humanist on behalf of his native land. More the politician, who had already shown in *Utopia* his interest in transatlantic discoveries and colonization, devoted himself entirely, in a manner totally different from his predecessor Wolsey, to maintaining England and the continent of Europe in peace. It was thus that he sought, in all loyalty, to serve his king, whose ambitions were bent upon the Continent. How thoroughly More was involved with secular power is most vividly shown to us in that picture transmitted by his son-in-law Roper: Henry VIII, an unexpected guest to dinner at Chelsea, walking for an hour with More in the garden, his arm about More's neck.

All this is Sir Thomas More, man of the world. Does not all this make him very unlike the picture of what one calls "a saint"? Can such involvement in the world be justified in terms of the Gospel? Can this be a following of Christ? Chris-

tian perfection? More's friend and instructor in Greek, Linacre, natural scientist and founder of the chairs of medicine
at Oxford and Cambridge, priest as he was and holder of many
ecclesiastical offices, came only late in life to open the New
Testament. He happened upon the Sermon on the Mount,
read the three chapters of Matthew with the utmost aston-
ishment, and cried out: "Either this is not the Gospel, or we
are not Christians." Was he not at least being consistent
when he threw the book away and immersed himself once
more in the study of medicine?

Living By the Gospel

But the question can be put the other way as well: To be a
true Christian, to live by the Gospel, to follow Christ, is it
enough to renounce all things and forsake the world? Does a
Christian, in short, need to become a monk if he is to be
saint?

What is indisputable is that it is quite possible for someone to renounce everything and live in the "state" of perfection, as given by the evangelical "counsels," and still be
anything but a saint. Why? Because the spirit is lacking. It
was often lacking in those days. Erasmus, in his *Praise of Folly*,
very clearly expressed his contempt for ignorant, immoral, un-
evangelical monks. The book was written in More's house and
with his encouragement. Flight from the world may well be
the product of weakness, inadequacy, disappointment or laziness. Flight from the world does not necessarily mean flight
to God. It can be a concealed flight back to the world; the
more and more worldly world of one's own ego.

But More saw the positive potentialities in monasticism

too, more clearly than Erasmus, who had, as a boy, been thrust into the cloister with no inner vocation whatsoever, and who had the greatest difficulty in obtaining a dispensation from his vow of obedience. The monasteries are the only European institution of which More's Utopians explicitly approve. Indeed, More had spent four years, while a law student, sharing the religious life of the London Carthusians. It is said that at this period he also contemplated becoming a Franciscan. He saw the positive potentialities in forsaking the world as an emphatic protest against the secularization of man and an explicit making room in man's life for God. Throughout his life, he never ceased to have a certain secret nostalgia for it. But after a long and searching examination he came to the conclusion that he was not made for the monastic life, not called to forsake the world.

Did this mean that More was giving up the idea of living by the Gospel and following Christ? To have a "state" of evangelical perfection without the *spirit* of evangelical perfection is not a possibility for a Christian. But could not a life in the *spirit* of evangelical perfection without the "state" be a genuine Christian possibility? What is the point of "the Gospel"? What is the good news of Jesus?

The message of Jesus is summed up in the words: "The time is accomplished, and the Kingdom of God is at hand" (Mark 1, 15). The reign of God is not yet present, but it is already breaking in. Its dawn is already manifesting itself. The appearance and work and teaching of Jesus are the sign of it. It is not men but God himself who is setting up his kingdom, his reign, by which all the sin and suffering of the world are taken away and the People of God, awaiting the fulfillment of the promises of the Prophets, is given the forgiveness of sins, the blessing of salvation:

> Blessed are ye poor;
> for yours is the Kingdom of God.
> Blessed are ye that hunger now:
> for you shall be filled.
> Blessed are ye that weep now:
> for you shall laugh.   (Luke 6, 20f.)

This message summons man to a decision: "Repent and believe the gospel!" (Mark 1, 15). Jesus himself, in his own person, signifies this demand from God for a decision: "Behold more than Solomon here. . . . Behold more than Jonah here" (Luke 11, 31f.). In Jesus' summons, it is the authoritative voice of God himself that speaks, before whom there can be no evasion. The choice is unambiguous and radical: God and his kingdom or the world and its goods. Neither family nor possessions nor public order can stand between a man and this radical decision between God and the world. Jesus himself forsook family, house and home. And he snatched away a little band of men from their families, houses and homes to go with him as his disciples. It is true he did not urge everyone to leave his family, house and home; Jesus was not a social revolutionary. But this he did do: he confronted every individual, every individual, with the radical decision of where he is going to set his heart; on God or on the goods of this world. Neither property nor family nor public order must keep a man from *setting his heart solely on God, the Lord, alone.*

Not property: "Lay not up to yourselves treasures on earth . . . for where thy treasure is, there is thy heart also" (Matt. 6, 19–21). "No man can serve two masters. For either he will hate the one, and love the other: or he will sustain the one, and despise the other. You cannot serve God and mammon"

(Matt. 6, 24). And how perilous is wealth: "How hardly shall they that have riches enter into the kingdom of God! . . . It is easier for a camel to pass through the eye of a needle, than for a rich man to enter into the Kingdom of God" (Mark 10, 23, 25). There is a warning against earthly cares: "Be not solicitous therefore, saying: What shall we eat, or what shall we drink, or wherewith shall we be clothed? For after all these things do the heathens seek. For your Father knoweth that you have need of all these things. Seek ye therefore first the kingdom of God and his justice, and all these things shall be added unto you" (Matt. 6, 31–3).

Not the family: "If any man come to me, and hate not his father, and mother, and wife, and children, and brethren, and sisters, yea and his own life also, he cannot be my disciple" (Luke 14, 26). "Do not think that I came to send peace upon earth: I came not to send peace, but the sword. For I came to set a man at variance against his father, and the daughter against her mother, and the daughter-in-law against her mother-in-law. And a man's enemies shall be they of his own household. He that loveth father or mother more than me, is not worthy of me; and he that loveth son or daughter more than me, is not worthy of me" (Matt. 10, 34–7).

Not public law and order: "You have heard that it was said to them of old. . . . But I say to you . . . !" (Matt. 5, 21–48). It is not only the commandments contained in the law that bind men; it is not only homicide, adultery and perjury that are against the commandment of God, but even anger, evil desire and untruthfulness. Above and beyond every formula of law, what God demands is man's whole will. But this means that he demands the abandonment of one's rights: "But I say to you not to resist evil: but if one strike thee on thy right cheek, turn to him also the other. And if a man will

contend with thee in judgment and take away thy coat, let go
thy cloak also unto him. And whosoever will force thee one
mile, go with him two" (Matt. 5, 39–41). This leads to the
reversal of all human rank: "You know that they who seem to
rule over the Gentiles, lord it over them: and their princes
have power over them. But it is not so among you: but whosoever will be greater, shall be your minister. And whosoever
will be first among you, shall be the servant of all" (Mark
10, 42–4).

This, then, is what is meant by following Christ: "If any
man will follow me, let him deny himself and take up his
cross and follow me" (Mark 8, 34). It is a radical decision:
"No man putting his hand to the plough and turning back, is
fit for the kingdom of God" (Luke 9, 62). Thus God wants
the whole of man; he wants his heart. Not so that man shall
abandon the world; Jesus sent his disciples out into the world.
But so that man shall be unhampered and free from the world,
totally in readiness. In readiness for what? For fulfilling God's
will, so as thus to be ready for the kingdom of God: "Whosoever shall do the will of God, he is my brother and my sister
and mother" (Mark 3, 35). What does God's will require?
Not merely a negative renunciation of the world, but a positive self-giving: love. No new commandments are formulated,
no new particular requirements laid down; there is only the
one completely concrete demand, which is at once quite unlimited and the answer to each individual case: " 'Thou shalt
love the Lord thy God with thy whole heart, and with thy
whole soul, and with thy whole mind.' This is the greatest and
the first commandment. And the second is like to this:
" 'Thou shalt love thy neighbor as thyself.' On these two
commandments dependeth the whole Law and the Prophets"
(Matt. 22, 37–40). What shows Christian perfection is the

love of enemies: "Love your enemies and pray for them that persecute you, that you may be the children of your Father who is in heaven, who maketh his sun to rise upon the good and bad and raineth upon the just and the unjust. . . . Be you therefore perfect, as also your heavenly Father is perfect" (Matt. 5, 44f., 48).

Who, then, is the follower of Christ, the man who is living perfectly by his Gospel? The man who, free from all worldly attachment, is always in readiness; readiness for God and God's demands, which he meets every day in his neighbor, in the everyday life of the world.

Thomas More was ready day by day. He had not given his heart to the goods of this world. He remained in the world but did not let himself be bound by it. He had preserved an ultimate independence from the world, and interior freedom for God. This comes out in all kinds of small matters.

Sir Thomas More delighted in his possessions, but was not subject to them. More, the man of the world, was no *bon vivant*. His inner superiority to the things of this world shows in his indifference in matters of appearance and of eating and drinking; he normally preferred simple fare to fine dishes. He was totally without greed or parsimony, gave freely of his wealth, and established an almshouse in Chelsea. This meant that after his resignation of the chancellorship he found himself in considerable straits. He was extremely anxious that his children, too, should be free from vanity. He tried to cure his daughter-in-law Anne Crisacre of it; when she asked him for a necklace of pearls he gave her—never at a loss for a joke—one of white peas. His inner freedom in regard to possessions comes out particularly strikingly on an occasion when, in his absence, his barns were destroyed by fire. He wrote to his wife Alice that she should compensate the neighbors to whose land the fire had spread: "For an I should not leave myself a spoon, there shall no poor neighbour of mine bear no loss by any chance happened in my house; I pray you be with my children and your household merry in God." His wife is to get a supply of corn for the household, and to decide whether they should keep the piece of land or not: "But I would not that any man were suddenly sent away, he wot ne'er wither." Thus More enjoyed his possessions, but his heart was given to God, the Lord, alone. How serious he was in his choice between God and possessions and in his radical readiness for God, the future was to show.

Sir Thomas More loved his family, but he was not wholly engrossed in the life of marriage and family. For all his delight in the atmosphere of his cultured family and in the rich community life lived in the circle of his wife and children and their numerous guests, More realized very well that this, so to say, horizontal dimension of human relationship is not the ultimately decisive thing; that, in everything, what matters is to be aware of the all-important vertical dimension of relationship with God. Thus More took good care that God should not be forgotten in the everyday life of his family. Hence he established a family life of prayer according to the forms of his day, and reading of the Scriptures in common. Every evening when the master of the house was at home, the whole household assembled for prayer. On Sundays and feasts they went to church, and on great feast-days all attended midnight Mass. More himself usually got up at two in the morning, and occupied himself with study and prayer until seven. He assisted at Mass every morning. Even when the King once sent for him repeatedly and urgently, he refused to come until Mass was over; Henry VIII took it in good part. During meals, a member of the family would read a chapter of Scripture with Nicolas of Lyra's commentaries. Not till this reading had been discussed was More's household fool allowed to lead the conversation into other paths. Thus More loved his family, but his heart was given to God, the Lord, alone. How serious he was in his choice between God and family and in his radical readiness for God, the future was to show.

Sir Thomas More greatly respected the law and the State, but for him they were not the highest thing. More devoted himself as few have done to the law, the kingdom and his king, but he preserved an inner detachment from it all, an overriding freedom. At the news that More had been summoned by the King to Court, Erasmus said somewhat ruefully: ". . . we shall get no more news from Utopia to make us laugh," and adds: "I know that More would rather laugh than be carried in official state." In fact, More avoids the Court as much as he can, as much as other men seek it. At the beginning of his courtier's life he wrote, in good humor, to Bishop Fisher: "Everybody knows that I didn't want to come to court, and the King often twits me about it; I sit as uneasily as a clumsy rider in the saddle." It was immediately after More had been made Under-Treasurer and knighted that he wrote the most sombre of all his books, the *Four Last Things:* the task of life is to meditate on death; the world, even for one who holds power and authority, is a prison, in which each prisoner is waiting to be led away to his execution:

> For if ye took the matter aright, the place a prison, yourself a prisoner condemned to death, from which ye cannot escape, ye would reckon this gear as worshipful as if a gentleman thief, when he should go to Tyburn, would leave for a memorial the arms of his ancestors painted on a post in Newgate. Surely, I suppose that . . . men would

bear themselves not much higher in their hearts for any
rule or authority that they bear in this world, which they
may well perceive to be indeed no better but one prisoner
bearing a rule among the remnant . . . or at the uttermost, one so put in trust with the gaoler that he is half
an under-gaoler over his fellows, till the sheriff and the
cart come for him.

Even when More had received, not just "any rule or authority" but the rule and authority of Lord Chancellor, he still
remained the same simple, unaffected, humble, selfless man
as before; as being, after the King, the highest in the State,
and therefore the servant of all. Sir Thomas dresses simply and
wears his gold chain only when it is absolutely necessary; he
takes no account of outward forms and loves equality and
freedom. None of his servants has ever fallen into disgrace.
His faithful secretary, John Harris, has the duty of pointing
out to him any mistake he may make. More is constantly
ready to help anyone as a matter of course: time, money, influence with the King and in high places is at anyone's disposal. With kind and merry conversation he knows how to
cheer the depressed and sorrowful. "You might call him the
general patron of all who are hard up." He himself makes no
demands on others. Lord Chancellor Wolsey once wrote to
the King of More that "he is not the most ready to speak and
solicit his own cause." And to Polydore Vergil, who thought
that More felt for some reason offended with him, Erasmus
wrote: "What you write about More is all nonsense; why, he
does not remember even grave injuries." More was capable of
loving his neighbor to the point of letting him have his cloak
as well as his coat, of going the two miles with him, of turning
the other cheek. Thus his respect for law and State was high,

but his heart was given to God, the Lord, alone. How serious he was in his choice between State and God and in his radical readiness for God, the future was to show.

In following this course, Thomas More was not moved by mere stoical indifference, but by convinced discipleship of Christ, which always involves self-denial and carrying the Cross. If his wife or one of his children was ill, he used to say: "We may not look at our pleasure to go to Heaven in feather beds: it is not the way, for our Lord himself went thither with great pain and by many tribulations, which was the path wherein he walked thither; for the servant may not look to be in better case than his master."

Henry VIII and his chancellor were both men of the world, and both wished to be Christians. Henry, who boldly proclaimed himself "sole protector and supreme head of the Church and clergy of England," appears as one who was enslaved to the world in the family, social and political spheres; sensuality, wealth and power were his idols, which he preferred before the Kingdom of God. It is not a question of judging Henry, but the difference between him and More shows clearly where the issue lies. To More, too, family, possessions and State meant much. But neither family nor wealth nor power were his idols. God alone was God for him. As a man of the world, taking an honest delight in the world, Sir Thomas sought to live in the world as a Christian, living according to the Gospel as a follower of Christ. He did it unostentatiously and without fuss. Who, looking at Holbein's portrait, would guess that this man, who looks so little like a "saint" and displays the costly furs of a man of the world, has long been wearing under them a rough hair-shirt—an object of scandal, perhaps, to many people today—which severely punished him, sometimes leaving blood on his clothes, and of which only his favorite daughter, Margaret, was supposed to know anything?

More important than such details is the fact that Thomas More, in his whole life in the world, put into practice those words of St. Paul which express, more perhaps than any others, the situation of a Christian in the world:

> They also who have wives be as if they had none; and they that weep as though they wept not; and they that rejoice as if they rejoiced not; and they that buy as though they possessed not; and they that use this world as if they used it not (1 Cor. 7, 29–31).

This is the freedom of a Christian living "in Christ," who lets the whole of his daily life be unostentatiously determined by Christ. This is the glad freedom of a Christian, which by God's grace is given to men in this world by faith. God, who is freedom itself, makes unfree man free, in Christ.

The Freedom of a Christian

Is the whole point, then, that a Christian should forsake the world and its goods? This is not the decisive thing. It is not even the normal thing. To forsake the world or any particular sphere within it is a charism of the Spirit that may well be bestowed on some particular individual, a special call from God affecting that particular individual. Thus Paul was given the charism of celibacy; an eschatological sign that the last times have begun—"The time is short" (1 Cor. 7, 29), "The fashion of this world passeth away" (1 Cor. 7, 31)—a sign visibly lifted up of the passing away of this world and the cre-

ation of the new man which has been achieved in Christ. Paul
glories in the charism of celibacy, but hastens to add: "But
every one hath his proper gift from God; one after this manner, and another after that" (1 Cor. 7, 7; cf. Matt. 19, 11f.).
According to Paul, it is not only these especially striking gifts
that are charisms of the Spirit, but all works of brotherly love:
"And having different gifts, according to the grace that is
given us, either prophecy, to be used according to the rule
of faith; or ministry, in ministering; or he that teacheth, in
doctrine; he that exhorteth, in exhorting" (Rom. 12, 6–8).

The Christian is to rejoice with them that rejoice and weep
with them that weep (Rom. 12, 15). He can enjoy this world
and its goods without fear or hypocrisy. Jesus himself, very
different in this from the ascetic John the Baptist, took part in
banquets and let himself be abused as "a glutton and a wine-
drinker" (Matt. 11, 19). He set a high value on marriage,
reasserted its indissolubility, and was tenderly affectionate toward children. He would not interfere in property matters, and
proposed no new distribution of wealth. He accepted the authority of the State and its right to levy taxes, and saw civic
duties in a positive light. Nor did Jesus want to cut his disciples off from the world. He did not want them, like the
Essenes, to dissociate themselves from the people and found
closed communities with a strict moral code. Nor did he want
them to form closed groups within the general community of
the people. He sent his disciples out into the world. Peter,
the brothers of the Lord and the other Apostles took their
wives with them when they went to preach the Gospel (1 Cor.
9, 5).

Many different ways lie open for Christian "perfection," the
perfect striving of a Christian existence toward God. The decisive thing for a Christian is not that he surrenders the goods

of this world, but that he does not surrender himself to them, does not give himself away to them, does not lose himself in them: neither in sex nor in wealth nor in power. A Christian can only surrender and give himself away to God, only lose himself in him, whom he has chosen, fundamentally and radically, in faith; God alone is absolute, all else is relative. Thus the decisive thing for a Christian is not that he abandons this world and its goods, but that he does not become enslaved to them. Putting it positively, that he preserves the glorious *freedom* of a Christian in respect of the world, a freedom which shows itself by interior *detachment* from the things of this world. The decisive thing is not an external, spatial detachment but an interior, personal one. Paul does not reject the "abundance" of this world; he knows how to live with it. But he preserves the overriding detachment of a free man, which makes him, in the last analysis, *indifferent* to abundance and to want: "I have learned, in whatsoever state I am, to be content therewith. I know both how to be brought low, and I know how to abound (everywhere and in all things I am instructed): both to be full and to be hungry; both to abound and to suffer need. I can do all things in him who strengtheneth me" (Phil. 4, 11–13). Such is the true, cheerful attitude of a Christian in the world; not the twisted rigidity of "having to sacrifice oneself," but what Paul calls "autarchy": sufficiency, freedom, in any situation.

A man enjoying this freedom is free from the anxiety of a man who is subject to the world, who lives under the "spirit of bondage" which necessarily leads to "fear" (Rom. 8, 15). A man who is a slave to the world is "solicitous"; "he is solicitous for the things of the world" (1 Cor. 7, 33), as though he could thus ensure himself a future. A man who is a slave of the world "covets"; he "covets evil things" (1 Cor. 10, 6), as though he could find rest and peace in the "works of the flesh." A man who is a slave to the world "glories in himself": he "glories" in his own strength and achievements and works (1 Cor. 4, 7), as though he had something which he had not received. A man who is a slave to the world "trusts in the flesh"; he "trusts in himself" (2 Cor. 1, 9), as though he could find stability in himself. This man, who has become enslaved to the world and its goods, who lives not only "in the flesh," but "according to the flesh," is involved in error; indeed, in sin. Instead of to the Creator of the world, he is handing himself over to the created world, seeking, in vain, to find in it the norm and the strength for his life; he thus falls into "enmity with God" (Rom. 8, 7).

But the Christian, who is not a slave to the world, but free as regards the world, is a servant or rather a child of God, is solicitous not for the things of the world, but "for the things that belong to the Lord" (1 Cor. 7, 32), and thus, in fact, for "nothing" (Phil. 4, 6). His desire is not for the works of the flesh but "to be with Christ" (Phil. 1, 23). He glories not in anything of his own but "in the Lord" (2 Cor. 10, 17), and hence in his own "infirmity" (2 Cor. 11, 30). He trusts, not in himself but "in God who raiseth the dead" (2 Cor. 1, 9). The Christian in the world is "not his own" (1 Cor. 6, 19), he belongs to God. He lives "not according to the flesh, but according to the spirit" (Rom. 8, 4); he clings not to what is visible, transitory and dying, but to the invisible, to the eternal, to life. He lives thus not for himself but for God, in "the freedom wherewith Christ has made us free" (Gal. 5, 1). This freedom does not consist in unrestrained, arbitrary willfulness, but in a new, joyful service of God and one's neighbor. Freedom implies a demand on us: "Be not conformed to this world: but be reformed in the newness of your mind, that you may prove

what is the good and the acceptable and the perfect will of
God" (Rom. 12, 2).

Thus the Christian takes to himself the great saying, "All
things are lawful to me" (1 Cor. 6, 12). But, "I will not be
brought under the power of any" (1 Cor. 6, 12). There is in
this world, indeed, "nothing that is unclean of itself" (Rom.
14, 14), neither in the family, the social nor the political
sphere, neither sex nor property nor power. But it is possible
for me to lose my freedom to something in the world, to let
myself be dominated by it, so that it becomes for me an idol.
Then we come up against the words, "All things are lawful to
me, but all things are not expedient" (1 Cor. 6, 12). More-
over, it is possible that what is in itself lawful to me, and even
expedient for me, may do damage to my neighbor. And then
the words that apply are, "All things are lawful for me, but all
things do not edify. Let no man seek his own, but that which
is another's" (1 Cor. 10, 23–4).

A Christian is at the service of others (1 Cor. 9, 19), but in
freedom: "Be not made the bond-slaves of men" (1 Cor.
7, 23). A Christian is not ultimately bound by any opinions,
judgments, assessments of value, conventions or traditions of
men: "For why is my liberty judged by another man's conscience?" (1 Cor. 10, 29). My own conscience, in its awareness
of good and evil, is what binds me (1 Cor. 8, 7–12; 10, 25–30).

The freedom of a Christian is freedom in the world, freedom from the world for God alone, in loving service of his
neighbor: in the family, the social and the political spheres.
This freedom is always demanded of a Christian in his enjoy-
ment of the world, always required of one who "uses this
world" (1 Cor. 7, 31). He must never lose himself in the
temptation of desiring to enjoy, to possess, to dominate; never

surrender to the demon of *eros* or of mammon or of power. He can love his wife and family, enjoy his possessions, act in the order of politics and law—all in freedom. But at any moment, this fundamental freedom of the Christian who uses this world may—for God, in the service of his neighbor—take on the form of *renunciation*. In renouncing the goods of this world the Christian is not renouncing his freedom. On the contrary, renunciation is what calls most fully upon his freedom and brings it into play to the maximum extent; this is how far I can go as a Christian, even to the point of free renunciation! It is when this maximum call is made on it that a Christian's freedom is *put to the test*. In renunciation, *here-and-now* renunciation, he shows of what quality his freedom has been, *everywhere and at all times*. This is where he shows that his free, radical choice of God in faith, often scarcely discernible in all the joys and sorrows and give-and-take of daily life, has not been an empty word, a high-sounding program, a pious ideal, a mere interior "intention," but a decisive act. It is in his practical here-and-now renunciation that a Christian gives proof that he is really a free man for God. The testings which call on a Christian to prove his freedom by renunciation are frequent; they come every day. How often a Christian has to give up *something* for the love of God, in service to his neighbor, in the family, social or political sphere!

But the *great* test of a Christian's freedom arises when he is faced with the choice of abandoning not just something but *everything* for the sake of God and his kingdom: of giving away "all that he has" to possess the field with the hidden treasure, the pearl of great price (Matt. 13, 44–6). The great test of a Christian's freedom arises when what is demanded of him is readiness not merely for some sort of renunciation, but for *total* renunciation. It was with this great test of freedom that Sir Thomas More was faced.

Death and Life

For a Christian who has radically chosen God and his kingdom in faith, so as to be ready for anything, this great test does not represent a break but a continuous advance in faith. For Thomas More, the great test did not involve a conversion, but a further putting into practice of that radical readiness in faith which he had maintained, in principle, through all his years as a student, lawyer, judge, diplomat and Lord Chancellor; readiness for anything, for any sacrifice. That fundamental readiness was now required to meet the fullest demands.

"*Indignatio principis mors est*, the wrath of the prince is death," said the Duke of Norfolk to More. "Is that all, my Lord?" was More's answer. "Then in good faith is there no more difference between your Grace and me, but that I shall die today and you tomorrow."

Thomas More could not follow a Henry VIII who, in pursuit of his matrimonial affairs, had declared himself, over and against the Pope, as "sole protector and supreme head of the Church and clergy of England." He tried to avoid the conflict and withdrew into private life; he tendered his resignation on "grounds of health." He did not seek martyrdom. He constantly insisted that he respected the consciences of those who thought differently from himself and would not try to dissuade them from their position. He said that he did not set himself up to judge the conscience, the loyalty or the wisdom of other men, but was only concerned with himself and what his own conscience commanded, adding that that same conscience brought to his mind so many imperfections of his past life that he could only implore God for mercy. But the freedom which he allowed to others was not granted to himself; he was accused of high treason.

It is not our business here to assess the justification for More's deciding against Henry. More was certainly no papal absolutist, no divinizer of the Papacy: "The Pope is a prince as you are. It may hereafter so fall out that Your Grace and he may vary upon some points, whereupon may grow breach of amity between you both." Such was his warning to Henry when the latter, in the first part of his reign, exaggerated the papal authority even in temporal matters. But More was equally certainly no royal absolutist, no divinizer of the monarchy: "And forasmuch as this indictment is grounded upon an Act of Parliament directly repugnant to the laws of God and his holy Church, the supreme government of which, or of any part whereof, may no temporal prince presume by any law to take upon him, as rightfully belonging to the See of Rome . . . it is therefore in law, amongst Christian men insufficient to charge any Christian man." Such were his words to the court that tried him, when Henry, in the second part of his reign, was setting aside the authority of the Pope in spiritual things. Whatever one's opinion is of More's decision, one cannot but respect it; it was the honorable decision, in conscience, of a believing Christian, who was ready to pay any price whatever for it: "Very and pure necessity, for the discharge of my conscience, enforceth me to speak so much. Wherein I call and appeal to God, whose only sight pierceth into the very depth of man's heart, to be my witness."

Now, when More's fundamental choice between God and the world is subjected to the ultimate test, this man of the world resolutely gives up *everything* for the known will of God.

He renounces his position in the State; he resigns office,

and gives back the Great Seal to the King. The man who was
England's chief statesman is thrown into the Tower.

He renounces his possessions; he loses his income, dismisses
those in his service, submits to the confiscation of his goods.
Poor, prematurely aged, and ill, leaning on a stick, the ex-Lord
Chancellor faces his judges.

He renounces his family: he says farewell to his wife and
children, who were eventually refused permission even to visit
him in prison. Complete loneliness has come upon the man
who signs his farewell letter to his Italian friend, Antonio
Bonvisi: "Thomas More: I should in vain put to it, 'Yours,'
for thereof can you not be ignorant, since you have bought it
with so many benefits. Nor now I am not such a one that it
forceth [= matters] whose I am."

To his favorite daughter, Meg, he admitted, while in prison,
the fear he felt: "Surely, Meg, a fainter heart than thy frail
father hath, canst thou not have. . . . And albeit I am of nature
so shrinking from pain, that I am almost afeared of a fillip, yet
in all the agonies that I have had . . . I thank the mighty mercy
of God, I never in my mind intended to consent, that I would
for the enduring of the uttermost, do any such thing as I
should in mine own conscience . . . think to be to myself such
as should damnably cast me in the displeasure of God." In his
fear he prayed that God would give him "the strength to take
it patiently, and peradventure somewhat gladly too." To his
friend Bonvisi he wrote a letter which was his farewell to the
international circle of his humanist friends: "And in the mean
season, Almighty God grant both you and me, good Master
Bonvisi, and all mortal men everywhere, to set at nought all
the riches of this world, with all the glory of it, and the pleasure of this life also, for the love and desire of that joy."

The following of Christ had become a literal reality for Thomas More. He wrote in prison: "Now to this great glory can there no man come headless. Our head is Christ: and therefore to him must we be joined, and as members of his must we follow him, if we will come thither. He is our guide to guide us thither. . . . Knew you not that Christ must suffer passion, and by that way enter into his kingdom? Who can for very shame desire to enter into the Kingdom of Christ with ease, when himself entered not into his own without pain?"

He drew his strength from the passion of Christ. He prepared for his end by writing a *Treatise on the Passion*. When he came to the words "they laid hands on him," his books and papers and everything he had with him in prison were taken from him. He had before been deprived for a time of writing materials, and had written a letter with a piece of charcoal: ". . . Of worldly things I no more desire than I have. . . . Written with a coal by your tender loving father, who in his poor prayers forgetteth none of you all. . . . And thus fare ye heartily well for lack of paper. Our Lord keep me continually true, faithful and plain."

And thus Sir Thomas More died as few have died before him or since; on the scaffold, cheerfully, with a smile, in the royal freedom of a Christian man. He prayed briefly for God's mercy, embraced the executioner, who begged his forgiveness, confessed his Catholic faith and called on all present to pray for the King, saying that he died "the King's good servant, but God's first." His last words were a joke about his beard, which he arranged on the block so that it should not be cut, since his beard at least had committed no treason.

Thomas More lost his life to save it. In him, the paradox of Christian living was visibly fulfilled:

We are reviled, and we bless:
We are persecuted, and we suffer it.
We are blasphemed, and we entreat.

(1 Cor. 4, 12f.)

As deceivers, and yet true:
as unknown, and yet known:
as dying, and behold we live:
as chastised, and not killed:
as sorrowful, yet always rejoicing:
as needy, yet enriching many:
as having nothing, and possessing all things.

(2 Cor. 6, 8–10)

Thomas More, in his secular dress, with his secular culture, in the midst of his family, his possessions, and his public life, was a saint. Not because he was without faults and sins; he had them, like every other human being, and he confessed them often before his death: "I have not been a man of such holy living as I might be bold to offer myself to death, and therefore put myself not forward, but drew back, lest God for my presumption might suffer me to fall. Howbeit, if God draw me to it himself, then trust I in his great mercy that he shall not fail to give me grace and strength." But, with all his sinfulness, he was a saint, because he, as a sinful man, chosen out and embraced by God's grace in Christ—"sanctified in Christ Jesus, called to be a saint" (1 Cor. i. 2)—made a radical choice of God, kept himself ready for God throughout his whole life in the world, and finally underwent the supreme test of that readiness in his death. Thus he knew the love of God in Christ, from which nothing can separate a man, neither life nor death:

> All things are yours . . . ,
> whether the world, or life, or death,
> or things present, or things to come:
> for all are yours;
> and you are Christ's:
> and Christ is God's. (1 Cor. 3, 22–3)

The example set forth before a Christian is such that it is possible for him, as a Christian, chosen out and embraced by God's grace in Christ, to live by the Gospel in the world; to follow Christ in the world, in the midst of his family and his possessions and the State; to live soberly, unsentimentally, honestly, unfanatically, unpietistically, seriously and at the same time joyfully: a holy life. What, then, is the real point for a Christian in the world? To make a radical choice in faith, despite all our sinfulness, and to sustain it through ordinary daily life, for God the Lord and his kingdom. To keep, in the world, one's fundamental freedom from the world, in the midst of one's family, one's possessions and the State, in service of God and of one's brothers. To be cheerfully ready at any time to embody this freedom in renunciation, even, when called on for it, in total renunciation. It is only in this freedom from the world, in the world, for God the Lord, given by God's grace, that the Christian can find strength, consolation, power, joy—victory.

2 THE FREEDOM OF THE CHURCH

For freedom Christ has set us free!
Stand fast therefore,
and do not submit again to a yoke of slavery!
Gal. 5, 1

The Church is the community of those who
have been called to the freedom of God, so
that her Law may be called the Law of Freedom. *Karl Rahner*

The Church Against Freedom?

In the summer of 1962, I was visited in Germany by an extremely friendly colleague from a famous American University, who asked me what the subject of my lecture in the United States was to be. I replied, "The Church and Freedom." "Very interesting," he said, with a charming smile. "I know that there's a Church, and I know that there's freedom, but I didn't know that you could have the Church and freedom together!"*

This remark, in its friendly way, puts the whole problem before us. Can we put an "and" in here at all: "The Church and Freedom"? Can one use it in a genuinely uniting way? Differently, that is, than when one speaks of "Communism and Freedom," meaning basically "Communism *versus* Freedom"? My American colleague was not a Christian, and his doubts would probably apply not only to the *Catholic* Church but to all Christian Churches. "The intolerance that spread over the world with the advent of Christianity is one of its most curious features," says Bertrand Russell in a book entitled *Why I am not a Christian.*†

* This chapter appeared originally in *Commonweal*, June 21, 1963, under the title "The Church and Freedom." Copyright © 1963 by Hans Küng.

† New York, Simon and Schuster, 1957.

obeying you and ruling only in your name. Again we shall be betraying them, for we shall not let you have anything to do with us any more." Indeed, "Why have you come to disturb us?" The Grand Inquisitor means to take this Jesus who has come again, bringing freedom once again, and burn him at the stake in the name of the Church.

This is a tremendous accusation. It is made, directly, against the Catholic Church. But to be honest it does not really only stand against her. Or were not heretics and witches burnt at the stake in Calvin's and Luther's Churches too, and were not opponents fought with violence instead of compelled by love? Does not everything of which the Catholic Church is accused in the way of lack of freedom, arbitrariness, authoritarianism and totalitarianism, exist in other shapes and forms, more or less disguised, among the Christians of other confessions, and indeed often more in small sects than in large Churches?

Now it is quite easy to protest against the accusations brought by Dostoevski and so many others, and say: that's one-sided, that's unfair, that is not the whole truth, that has to be understood in relation to the period, and it is all to be found outside the Church too. Certainly; Dostoevski himself admits it. But this answer does not meet the accusation. Nor is it a Christian answer. Would it not be more Christian, more in accordance with the spirit of Christ's Gospel, if when wanting to make some highly problematical defense of ourselves we did not immediately start looking for the mote in our neighbor's eye and working out some kind of tortuous, white-washing apologetics? Would it not be, in fact, a proof that Christian *freedom* does, in spite of everything, remain amongst us, if we—we Christians of all confessions—found the courage to say, soberly and without covering up, that, alas, there have on innumerable occasions been sins against the freedom of the children of God committed in our Church, and that they are committed to this day?

Blots on Church History

In America, because of the young but great tradition of this country, there will be fewer inhibitions than in Europe against admitting this in an honest, realistic, Christian way. Since the first French Huguenots and Puritans and Pilgrims and again since the immigration of the brave Irish Catholics who had suffered so much, countless religious dissenters have poured into this great American land of freedom because, in their Catholic or Protestant lands of origin, they were often in an appalling way oppressed, harassed and persecuted.

The blot upon Church history is there: scarcely had the Church got her own period of persecution behind her when she began to come out in favor of persecuting those of other faiths: Arians, Donatists, Manichees in the early period, Catharists, Albigenses, Waldenses and Templars in the Middle Ages. Great theologians (Optatus, Leo I, Thomas Aquinas) defended the death penalty for heresy. In the modern period, Christians have persecuted Jews and Moors, Catholics have persecuted Protestants, and Protestants Catholics.

The Inquisition, in particular, with its appalling trials, confiscation of goods, imprisonments, tortures and countless death sentences, cannot be justified in any way whatever, however we try to understand it in terms of the circumstances of the time. It was not the Reformation but the Enlightenment that put an end to it in its crudest forms. What is bad is that even today the spirit of the Inquisition and unfreedom has not died out.

Every manifestation in the Church of lack of freedom, however harmless, however much under cover, whatever religious trimmings it may have, contributes toward making the Church less believable in the eyes of the world and of men in general; and that is a miserable disaster. For is it not true that whatever manifestation of unfreedom there may be in the Church is not a revelation of the good, luminous *nature* of the Church, but of her dark, evil *unnature?*

The Church, being a Church made of men and a Church made of sinful men, is not simply taken out of the unfreedom of this world. But her most intimate nature, her whole meaning and purpose—utterly unlike Communism, which does not acknowledge the freedom and dignity of the individual, and makes an idol of the collective—this whole purpose of hers is not unfreedom but freedom, the glorious freedom of the children of God. According to her external unnature, the Church may in many ways resemble Communism in its enslavement of men. In her inner nature she is radically the opposite pole from that pseudo-Church with its pseudo-faith. In her inner nature she is, despite all external signs to the contrary, the dwelling place of freedom.

Church as Dwelling Place for Freedom

The history of the West—and the history of America in particular—has from its beginnings been shaped by the idea of freedom; it was not without reason that the English historian, Lord Acton, planned to write the whole history of the West as a "History of Liberty." Without the Church of Christ, that history is unthinkable.

There was a preparation for the Christian understanding of freedom in the understanding of freedom among the Greeks. Again and again the Greeks sought to answer the question:

Who is free? But they did not escape the two extremes: that was on the one hand asceticism, i.e., a maximum of abstinence regarding this world's goods (food, drink, sexuality, etc.), and on the other hand libertinism, i.e., a maximum lack of restraint in the life of this world.

Christian freedom is neither ascetic nor libertine. It is meant to be realized in community, in the Church. It is true that, as St. Paul says, this Christian community has its home in Heaven (Phil. 3, 20), and is waiting for that higher, free Jerusalem, the holy polis, to come down from Heaven (Gal. 4, 26; cf. Heb. 12, 22; Apoc. 3, 12, etc.). But the Church is not a colony of heavenly citizens on earth taking no interest in the condition of the world. Rather, she takes part—though from a level that gives detachment—in the affairs and dealings of this world (1 Cor. 7, 29–31), rejoices with the joyful and weeps with them that weep (Rom. 12, 15). Not only is she to observe obedience, binding in conscience, toward the secular power (Rom. 13, 1–7); she is also herself to build up social life, by settling herself her own various conflicts (1 Cor. 5–7) and by doing this in constructive love, not limited to her community but unlimited (1 Cor. 8–14).

It is this active love of one's neighbor in the world, for the sake of the world, springing from the love of God, that reveals the freedom of Christians and of their community. This freedom is as far removed from all asceticism hostile to the world as from all libertinism in subjection to the world (1 Cor. 6, 12–20; cf. 1 Pet. 2, 16).

Thus the Church which proclaims the Gospel of Jesus is meant to bring men freedom, true freedom. It is not that freedom which man thinks he can win for himself. Man in the concrete is not in fact the Stoic's ideal, purely rational being, capable of following the law of reason. It is all too easy for man to conceal from himself the fact that he is not, at bottom, that sovereign free person that he likes to pose as being. Unless he wants to shut his eyes to the gloomy reality about him, he keeps finding himself a prisoner: chained to the objects and goods and forces of this world, chained above all to himself, that self which he has made so far. "For to will is present with me," says St. Paul, "but to accomplish that which is good, I find not. For the good which I will, I do not; but the evil which I will not, that I do. . . . I find then a law, that when I have a will to do good, evil is present with me. . . . Unhappy man that I am, who shall deliver me from the body of this death?" And the apostle gives the answer proclaimed by the Church: "Thanks be to God, by Jesus Christ our Lord!" (Rom. 7, 18–25).

How, indeed, is man to pull himself out of the swamp of his own unfreedom by the hair of his own head? How is he himself to wipe out his own servile, sinful self and attain a new, free self? No, do not let us deceive ourselves: man himself does not make himself truly free. But it is as St. Paul says with the utmost clarity: "Christ has set us free unto freedom" (Gal. 5, 1). Or, in St. John's Gospel: "If therefore the Son shall make you free, you shall be free indeed" (John 8, 36).

In Christ, God himself has freely given himself to men; in Christ, God himself has created man for himself, free and open to God. In him, access is granted and created for all men to this new, true freedom. To man, thinking that his freedom consists in being independently subject to himself, the announcement is made that he can only attain to freedom by letting himself be subject to another; not to men, who debase him to slavery, but to God, who raises him up to be his own free child. The *illusion* of freedom is to do what I want. The *reality* of freedom is to want what Almighty God does.

Thus the ground and source of man's freedom lies, not in man himself, who is by nature the slave of sin, but in the freedom of God, in the freedom of his grace setting us free in Christ. This new freedom of God in Christ is made present in the Church through all ages by the Spirit. The Spirit, the Spirit of life in Christ Jesus, has set us free from the law of sin and death (Rom. 8, 2): "Where the Spirit of the Lord is, there is liberty" (2 Cor. 3, 17). In the Spirit, Christ calls us and illuminates us to freedom by his word. "For you, brethren, have been called unto liberty," says Paul (Gal. 5, 13; cf. 1 Cor. 7, 21–24; John 8, 31f.). In the Spirit, Christ awakens us and makes us alive to freedom through the sign of baptism: "So do you also reckon," says Paul to the baptized Christians, "that you are dead to sin, but alive unto God in Christ Jesus our Lord" (Rom. 6, 11).

This is the freedom of God in Christ, proclaimed and given to men through the Spirit in the Church, in her word and her sacraments, and which streams out thence, unchecked by any church walls, into the whole of humanity, which is already, as a whole, even though it does not know it, embraced by the liberating grace of God in Christ. This freedom is not an empty, formal freedom *from* something. Freedom for what? That is the question, the question that touches the meaning of freedom. The Church answers this question in her proclamation of the message of Christ to men. Freedom from the slavery of sin—for what? Freedom for the saving grace of God! Freedom from the oppressive constraint of the law—for what? Freedom for the Gospel, the Good News of the reign of God and the salvation of men in faith and service of their neighbor. Freedom from the destroying power of death—for what? Freedom for life, for eternal life in the glory of God.

Is this not a marvelous message of freedom, which the

Church of Christ is allowed to announce to the world? Is it not a glorious freedom, this freedom of the sons of God which, already now hidden in the Church, by God's grace, as a pledge, a matter of hope, is to become reality? For all those who are driven by the Spirit of freedom are sons, children of God (Rom. 8, 14f.). "And if sons, heirs also, heirs indeed of God and joint heirs with Christ: yet so if we suffer with Him, that we may be also glorified with Him. For I reckon that the sufferings of this time are not worthy to be compared with the glory to come, that shall be revealed in us" (Rom. 8, 17–18). For then will be revealed, as Paul says, "the freedom of the glory of the children of God" (Rom. 8, 21).

But precisely in the certainty of hope for this glory still to be revealed, Paul, and the Church with him, can already, in all the distress and anxiety of this world, rejoice over our God-given freedom:

If God be for us, who is against us? . . . Who shall separate us from the love of Christ? Shall tribulation, or distress, or famine, or nakedness, or danger, or persecution, or the sword? . . . But in all these things we overcome because of Him that hath loved us. For I am sure that neither death, nor life, nor Angels, nor principalities, nor powers, nor things present, nor things to come, nor might, nor height, nor depth, nor any other creature shall be able to separate us from the love of God which is in Christ Jesus our Lord (Rom. 8, 31–39).

Such is the glorious freedom of the children of God, and the Church is there to be the dwelling place for it. And this freedom in the Church is not just an empty assertion, not a mere theory or a beautiful ideal; it is—though only, indeed, for those who believe—a reality. It is true that to someone who is simply examining the Church critically from outside, her walls may well seem more like the walls of a fortress or even a prison than those of a sanctuary of the free Holy Spirit. It is true, too, that even someone looking at the Church from within keeps noticing afresh the lack of freedom in every nook and corner of her: servility pretending to be obedience and cowardice pretending to be prudence; power politics masking itself as spiritual service, and dishonesty as defense of the truth. Above all, he notices at every level, low and high, a constantly recurring, appalling, cowardly, worldly fear: a fear by which all Christian responsibility, courage, boldness, initiative, all Christian freedom, is in so many people struck dead and buried.

There is this unfreedom within the Church—as indeed the world always will exist within the Church. This unfreedom is not to be defended, whitewashed, or dismissed as harmless. The only thing to be asserted is that it is not the decisive thing. The decisive thing is the freedom of the Gospel of Jesus Christ, for which the Church really is the dwelling place: a freedom which countless Christians since the apostolic Church have, for all their failures, grasped in faith and obedience and humility, lived in love and in joy, suffered in hope and patience, fought for and prized. In all the great and small crises of life, in—as St. Paul says—distress, fear, persecution, hunger, nakedness, danger and death, it was by the power of this freedom of Jesus Christ that countless people in the Church and beyond her limits have over and over again been given support, comfort, strength, hope, joy and peace.

The Christian idea of freedom has also had effects upon world history: in the demand made in face of the Roman Empire for freedom to confess the faith, to proclaim it, and to worship; in the patient endurance of persecution, strengthened by countless martyrdoms, from Roman imperial times down to the present day; in the Church's struggle for her independence against the Caesaro-papist Byzantine emperors, the theocratic emperors of the Middle Ages and the absolutist rulers of modern history; in the struggle of the Reformers for freedom of conscience, of preaching and of worship; and finally even in the ideas of the Enlightenment on tolerance and freedom of conscience (which were, on the other hand, to a large extent shaped by thought on the lines of Stoicism and the natural law), leading to constitutional and legal results especially in the United States, in England and in France.

These historical effects of the Christian idea of freedom are of course of great importance. But in many respects, especially when they were linked, as in the Middle Ages, with a claim to worldly power on the part of the Church, they are very problematical. They could not be decisive for the Church. The Church, rightly understood, is not in her essence some sort of higher order of political system or pressure group, with definite tactical aims over against the State and society. Nor is she a bureaucratic machine with an army of officials, whose effectiveness can be measured sociologically.

In her essence the Church is the community of those who believe and love through Christ, who, despite any phenomena of unfreedom, strive unostentatiously—and in ways that history can only very indirectly take account of—to work out their royal freedom in everyday life by service to their neighbor for God's sake. This freedom can be realized in time of persecution or toleration, under any form of state or society. This freedom of the children of God is not something effected in the Church by society, or the State, or human beings, but something given from above, by God in Christ through his

Spirit. This freedom in the Church is a gift of God's grace; but for just this reason it is a task for the people in the Church.

The Task of Freedom

Freedom in the Church always has to be won over and over again. This is equally an important matter and a difficult one. The realization of freedom in the Church is a task of decisive *importance:* How is the Church with her message of freedom to be regarded as credible by men if she herself does not show herself as a dwelling place of freedom? How is she to show herself as a dwelling place of freedom unless freedom shines out everywhere through her institutions and constitutions, her ministries and ordinances? It is of decisive importance that the Church's free nature should not be impenetrably covered and displaced in men's eyes by her unfree unnature. No talking, no preaching, no theologizing about freedom in the Church can have any effect without there being free life in the Church.

Even in St. Paul's time the freedom of a Christian man did not consist only in a new relationship of the person to God; it also had an ecclesiological application. So St. Paul came out energetically for the free life of the Church, for freedom as lived by the individual and the individual community: against the traditionalist legalism of the Judeo-Christians, who wanted to impose on the Gentile Christians their legal prescriptions from the Mosaic law (Galatians); and also against the arrogance of people who passed judgment on the personal decisions of others in faith and conscience (Rom. 14; 1 Cor. 8 and 10). More than ever today in this century of totalitarianism the Church must avoid suggesting even the merest appearance of being a form of totalitarianism, authoritarianism and absolutism with a religious coloring to it.

The realization of freedom in the Church is an extraordinarily *difficult* task. It would be simple if she only had to fight for her freedom outwards, against the unfreedom of the world. It would be simple if only the Church were not, in her human activity, always a piece of the world herself. The very same institutions and constitutions, ministries and ordinances which according to their nature are meant to serve the freedom of the children of God can, against their nature, through the failures and sinfulness of men, be misused to bring about servitude. The front in the battle between freedom and unfreedom runs through the middle of the human heart, through the middle of the Church with her institutions and constitutions. The threat to freedom from within is very much more dangerous and very much more difficult to fight than the threat from without. When freedom is threatened by the world outside, the Christian can find protection, refuge and freedom within the Church, the community of those who are truly free. When freedom is threatened from within, inside the Church herself, the Christian can only find protection, refuge and freedom alone in himself, in the fortress of his own free conscience.

We do not by any means only have to think of extreme cases such as Galileo and St. John of the Cross in the hands of the Inquisition or St. Joan of Arc at the stake. We have to think of all those countless, unnamed scientists, philosophers, theologians, politicians, etc., who have been brought into the most severe conflicts of conscience because certain representatives of the Church did not preserve the limits set them by the freedom of all the children of God, because they mixed up the revelation of God with some ideology, over-

stepped their competence and involved themselves in questions purely scientific, philosophical, political, economic. . . .
How sad, how tragic it is that in our own modern times countless people have fled from the Church, the place of freedom,
to seek freedom in the world. More than ever today, when
freedom is so sorely threatened from without and from within,
must the Church strive to be, in freedom, a hospitable home
for all men of good will.

However, it must not be an illusion of freedom but true
freedom that is realized in the Church. Willfulness is only
the illusion of freedom, the willfulness of doing just what one
fancies. The willfulness of the individual, setting himself up
as his own God and thus handing himself over to all the
demons of his lust and passions, to all the spirits of the age
and movements of the age, to all the forces of the natural and
historical process, is merely another form of unfreedom. The
absolutism of the individual, like the absolutism of the many,
means servitude and tyranny. Was not the Jacobin Reign of
Terror in the French Revolution set up in the name of liberty
and equality? Even the Greeks knew that true freedom is only
granted to man when he is bound to the nomos, the law recognized and assented to in its inner meaning.

For the Christian this nomos is "the law of the Spirit of
life in Christ" (Rom. 8, 2), which frees man, till then unfree
and closed within himself, opening him to God and men in
love. The Church as the community of those who believe
and love wants to provide man with a place within which he
can work out his freedom under grace. Under Christ and his
Spirit the Church herself is by no means given over to the
willfulness of the individual believer and chance; she is not a
wild, disordered, anarchical congregation. We are obliged to
say this clearly to our Protestant brothers. Under Christ and

his Spirit the Church has a form, a shape, an articulation, a ministry, an authority, in short, an order: order in her preaching, her worship, her leadership.

The Church of the New Testament is not a disordered but an ordered society with her creed, her Baptism and Lord's Supper, and her authorities. She is an ordered community of prayer, love and action. In the concrete, the order and constitution of the first individual Christian communities were certainly very various, and one must beware of transferring the order and constitution of the original community at Jerusalem to the order of the Pauline community at Corinth. But St. Paul himself, the great apostle of freedom, in his letters to that very community of Corinth, rejected disorderly enthusiasm. For him, too, order includes authority, the power of leadership, and he himself—entirely in the service of the community—asserted it very decisively (1 Cor. 4, 21): in what he lays down for the exclusion of the incestuous man (1 Cor. 5), on mixed marriages and the unmarried (1 Cor. 7), on the liturgy (1 Cor. 11), on speaking with tongues and speaking under inspiration (1 Cor. 14). It is just at this point that he brings in the foundation for his setting things in order: "For God is not the God of dissension, but of peace" (1 Cor. 14, 33). And hence the requirement: "But let all things be done decently and according to order" (1 Cor. 14, 40). St. Paul appeals explicitly to an authority, a power which the Lord has given him for the building up of the community (2 Cor. 10, 8; 13, 10).

It is only a short step from this to the saying, transmitted in various forms in the Gospels: "He that hears you, hears Me: and he that despises you, despises Me. And he that despises Me, despises Him that sent Me" (Luke 10, 16; cf. Matt. 10, 40; John 13, 20). Seen from this viewpoint, there is no need to set the more charismatically inclined Pauline concept of the Church in exclusive opposition to the more institutional concept in the Acts of the Apostles and the Pastoral Epistles.

Freedom in the Church, then, cannot be willfulness of the individual but only freedom in order. True, every institution and constitution, every office and ministry, every doctrine and ruling, every ordinance and admonition, every censure and punishment, belong to the age that is passing away; all of this is to be sustained in the Church by the spirit of love, and is to serve the freedom of the sons and daughters of God. But it is all to be taken seriously as an expression of the Church's order. Just as there can be no true order in the Church without true freedom, so there can be no true freedom in the Church without order! Anyone who, through dictatorship and terror, destroys freedom in the Church also destroys true order and authority in the Church. And anyone who, through rebellion and revolt, destroys order and authority in the Church also destroys true freedom in the Church. Both freedom in order and order in freedom make up the Church of Christ.

The Churches which sprang from the Reformation have, because of their historical situation, laid the stress primarily on *freedom* in order; the Catholic Church, on the basis of her tradition, primarily on *order* in freedom. Today, in the age of ecumenical encounter, we are seeing on both sides that we can learn from each other. The Churches of the Reformation and their theology—constantly threatened by subjectivism and pseudo-mystical enthusiasm—are concerning themselves today in a new and positive way with the structure of the Church, with questions of authority, warrant and constitution, in short, with order in the Church.

The Catholic Church and her theology—constantly threatened by externalized, legalistic authoritarianism—are concerned today in a new and positive way with the personal responsibility of the individual Christian in relation to the Church, with the meaning of the charismatic gifts of the Spirit in relation to office, of the laity in relation to the clergy, of the local church in relation to the universal Church, in short, with freedom in the Church.

In face of the Protestant emphasis on freedom it was a thankless task in the Catholic Church for pope and bishops to emphasize the importance of authority and instruction. But it was a very necessary task, necessary also in relation to the Protestant churches, which have always been in danger of getting lost in subjectivism and individualism. To an American Protestant theologian complaining about the inactivity of many Protestant communities because, as he thought, of the too strong position of the ministry, I had to answer: a weak ministry cannot strengthen the community, a strong ministry can!

When we compare the situation with the Catholic Church, may not the inactivity of many Protestant communities be due in fact to the weak position of the Protestant ministry? Certainly, we do not ask for authoritarianism and clericalism, which in fact would not strengthen but weaken the ministry. On the contrary, we ask for freedom. And we have to do it now frankly, honestly and concretely. When we thus call for freedom in the Catholic Church, we believe that in fact we do not undermine but fortify authority and order. In this sense we shall now look at some concrete manifestations of Church freedom in the *Catholic* area—manifestations that have in part been realized, and in part still need to be realized. If this is done frankly and honestly, it will be at once an invitation and a challenge to our Protestant brethren, not to maintain their positions, inactively and proudly, appealing to the Reformation as something already accomplished, but to examine their own positions, so as to come courageously to meet us, by taking stock of concrete manifestations of Church order, both realized and potential.

A Catholic stock-taking of manifestations of freedom in the Church can take place much more easily, much more convincingly, much more cheerfully today than would have been possible some years ago. Why? Because we have behind us the final session of the Second Vatican Council, preparations for which had given rise to many fears for freedom in the Church. However, it is not the fears, but the hopes that have been fulfilled: the Second Vatican Council has itself become a manifestation of freedom in the Church observed by the whole world. This was no totalitarian party congress, but thanks to the energy and boldness of the bishops, it became a Council of spontaneous initiatives, frank discussions and independent decisions. Is it an illusion to hope that with this Council a new period has begun in the history of the Catholic Church: the period of a new and fruitful freedom in the Church?

And is it an illusion to hope that the Catholic Church of the United States of America will take an important, a leading position in this new period, this "New Frontier" of the Catholic Church? Before coming to America, I studied the history of the U.S.A. more closely than I had before. What adventurous courage, what inexhaustible force and what magnificent generosity come out in this story of a dynamism never seen in the world before, a dynamism which was essentially formed by the idea of freedom!

The Catholic Church in the U.S.A. has her share in that story. She has done mighty pioneer work in the most various fields. What might it mean for the people of the United

States on the one hand and for the universal Catholic Church on the other, if this Church of the United States would now prove herself as having the same courage, the same energy, the same magnificence on the "New Frontier" of the Catholic Church, in this period of a new, ecumenically-minded freedom, which goes out not to conquer others but to meet with them? And that she will so prove herself, I have no doubt at all, having met so many open-minded American bishops and theologians at the Council. Even before the Council was a few weeks old, there had already accumulated many signs, in the U.S.A. in particular, of a new life in the Church. The question now becomes all the more pressing: Where and how, in the concrete, does freedom show itself in the Church?

Right from the start, I am going to leave aside one whole complex of questions in which I do not feel competent, because of the different situation in the U.S.A.: that is, the relation between Church and State. All the same, there are two things calling for grateful acknowledgement: 1. On this particular point, there are essential insights for which European theology has to thank American theologians, especially John Courtney Murray, S.J., who has seen how to make a theoretical interpretation of the constitutional separation of Church and State in a positive and constructive sense; 2. At the practical level too the United States has given the world an outstanding example of how Church and State can work together for the good of the people in mutual independence and respect.

We too can be sure of this much: State and Church flourish best when they do not seek to reduce each other to subservience but when they leave each other the greatest possible freedom. What this means fundamentally for the individual person is the recognition of religious freedom, both by Church

and by State. And this brings us to the first concrete point at
which freedom in the Church can and should be manifest. We
can only touch briefly on three individual points.

Freedom of Conscience

In the course of centuries, many faults have been committed by and in the Catholic Church against freedom of conscience. Even Paul, as we have seen, had to make a stand for
freedom of conscience in the Church, and many others have
had to do it since, with, of course, varying degrees of success.
But in modern times, with the growth of pluralist societies,
the sense of freedom of conscience in the Catholic Church too
has grown stronger and clearer. In its *Declaration on Religious
Liberty* the Second Vatican Council said:

> In faithfulness therefore to the truth of the Gospel,
> the Church is following the way of Christ and the apos-
> tles when she recognizes, and gives support to, the prin-
> ciple of religious freedom as befitting the dignity of man
> and as being in accord with divine revelation.
> . . . In the life of the people of God as it has made
> its pilgrim way through the vicissitudes of human history,
> there has at times appeared a way of acting that was
> hardly in accord with the spirit of the Gospel or even
> opposed to it. Nevertheless, the doctrine of the Church
> that no one is to be coerced into faith has always stood
> firm.
> Thus the leaven of the Gospel has long been about its
> quiet work in the minds of men, and to it is due in great
> measure the fact that in the course of time men have

come more widely to recognize their dignity as persons, and the conviction has grown stronger that the person in society is to be kept free from all manner of coercion in matters religious.*

This does not only exclude brutal, external force but also subtle, undercover, indirect force and pressure. In the few countries, such as Spain, where there is still not full freedom of conscience, religion and worship, it should be demanded energetically from the Catholic side. In the last few years one has already noted some advances.

A very significant sign of the change that has taken place was the statement made by Augustin Cardinal Bea, President of the Secretariat for Christian Unity: "As one . . . distortion of the love of truth falsely understood, there were those agonizing religious wars, when men tried in the name of truth to impose certain convictions on others by means of force, forgetting something that is no less fundamental than the love of truth: that is, human freedom. This freedom consists in man's right to decide perfectly freely on his own destiny in accordance with his own conscience. Out of this freedom spring the duty and the right of man to follow his own conscience. Corresponding to this right and duty there is the duty of the individual and of society to respect this freedom and self-determination."

In answer to the objection sometimes made in certain circles that "Error has no right to exist," he said: ". . . all we need to bring against this is that error is an abstraction and hence cannot be the subject of a right. It is rather the person who has a right, even when he is in invincible error, meaning

---

* Second Vatican Council's *Declaration on Religious Liberty*, 12.

that he is unable to correct his error. He thus has the duty and the right to follow his conscience, and thus also has a right to have this independence of his respected by all."

This viewpoint was confirmed by the Second Vatican Council. Concerning freedom of conscience, the Council declares:

> Truth, however, is to be sought after in a manner proper to the dignity of the human person and his social nature. The inquiry is to be free, carried on with the aid of teaching or instruction, communication and dialogue, in the course of which men explain to one another the truth they have discovered, or think they have discovered, in order thus to assist one another in the quest for truth.
>
> Moreover, as the truth is discovered, it is by a personal assent that men are to adhere to it.
>
> On his part, man perceives and acknowledges the imperatives of the divine law through the mediation of conscience. In all his activity a man is bound to follow his conscience, in order that he may come to God, the end and purpose of life. It follows that he is not to be forced to act in a manner contrary to his conscience.*

What has been said here about freedom of conscience applies equally, of course, to dogma. Dogma does not violate the conscience, it respects it. Certainly we are convinced that there is no real conflict between our conscience and the dogma of the Church. But what is also true is that a Christian has never to accept a dogma of the Church if it would be against his conscience. Naturally none of this is a demand either for the relativizing of all truth or for a revolution against the existing

* Second Vatican Council's *Declaration on Religious Liberty*, 3.

order in the Church; but it is a call for maturity of conscience in every Christian and for respect for freedom of conscience in every human being. If the Church stands for the individual's freedom of conscience, there will be more readiness to listen to her when she stands for truth and when she gives her message of freedom; and the obligations that she lays on men will be accepted both more seriously and more gladly.

Freedom of Speech

The virtue of prudence has often been falsified in the Church in a very time-serving way: made to mean being careful only to say what is opportune, i.e., what is pleasing to those in charge. This meant overlooking the fact that in the New Testament caution plays only a small role, frankness a large one. The Greek word *parresia* is so often used there, in the sense of the openness that does not hush up or conceal anything, of the frankness that feels no embarrassment, of the boldness that has no fear. In apostolic frankness, at Antioch, Paul "withstood Peter to the face" (Gal. 2, 11), because he "dissimulated" and "did not walk uprightly unto the truth of the gospel" (2, 13f.). We are to stand for the Gospel when it is opportune or inopportune, "in season and out of season," according to the second Epistle to Timothy (4, 2) which is always read precisely on the feasts of Doctors of the Church.

The witness of freedom of speech in the Church has been borne by Irenaeus against Pope Victor, Jerome against Pope Damasus, Columban against Boniface IV, Bernard of Clairvaux against Eugene III, Bridget of Sweden against Gregory XI, Philip Neri against Clement III; and by so many other saints like Catherine of Siena, Thomas More, Robert Bellar-

mine. . . . It was Gregory the Great who said, "But if scandal
is taken at the truth, it is better to allow scandal to arise than
to neglect the truth" (*In Ezech. Hom.* 7, P.L. 77,324). And
Thomas Aquinas stressed the necessity for free criticism, *cor-
rectio fraterna*, even to ecclesiastical superiors (*Summa Theol.*
II–II, q. 33, a. 1–4).

It was not till modern times that the Catholic Church has
been put on the defensive by the Reformation, Gallicanism,
the Enlightenment, the French Revolution, Liberalism and
Socialism. And it was supposed to be a service to the Church
to cut down free speech and free writing as far as possible.
The fact that advance censorship of books was introduced by
the Renaissance Popes Innocent VIII, Alexander VI and
Leo X, and the centralized Index of Prohibited Books by
the extremist ex-Grand Inquisitor Caraffa, Paul IV (1559),
is not exactly the best possible recommendation for these
measures.

Absolutist methods, which have disappeared in the civil
sphere along with absolutist rulers, thus to some extent pro-
long their anachronistic existence within the Catholic Church.
Though Leo XIII had prepared the way in his Encyclical
Libertas, it was not till Pius XII that we had any clear word
on the necessity for a free public opinion in the Church. But
the Second Vatican Council not only made a reality of free
discussion in the Church in a way that had been simply unknown in more recent times, but also in its own proceedings
provided impressive proof that free speech and constructive
criticism do not weaken the Church but strengthen her.

Both inside and outside the Catholic Church there is hope
that we will go fearlessly on along this road. It would be a
magnificent manifestation of freedom if we would take those
repressive institutions—which the Church got along very well

without for fifteen hundred years and which are unquestionably out of date today—and boldly and confidently abolish
them all. I refer, firstly, to the *Index of Prohibited Books;*
secondly, to the advance censorship of religious books. Pope
Paul has already begun this type of needed reform by abolish-
ing Roman inquisitorial proceedings, in which denunciations
are accepted, in which the accusers, the evidence, the order of
procedure and all the acts are kept secret, in which the accused
is not given a hearing, those who defend him are not admitted,
and sentence is passed without stating the grounds for the
judgment; if I am not mistaken, such methods offend not only
against the Gospel but against the natural law which is so
often being quoted.

It is urgently necessary that the Church today should clearly
repudiate the methods of the totalitarian state. If in many
fields, such as exegesis, history of dogma, comparative religion,
etc., the Catholic Church still lags far behind Protestant
theology, this lamentable fact is not due to a lack of intelligence or unreadiness to work on the part of Catholic theologians, but to lack of freedom.

Certainly freedom, like so much that is good, is a dangerous
thing. And more freedom in the Church means that the demand on the individual priest, theologian, layman is not for
less but for more sense of responsibility, not for less but for
more sense of order and authority, not for less but for more
sense of genuine, free obedience. But the Catholic Church
of today is surely ripe for all this. And it would be precisely
in this renewal of freedom in speech and writing that she
would represent a challenge to the Protestant Churches to
investigate the question of true authority and order in the
Church, true order in the creed, in theology and in the life of
the Church.

Freedom of Action

It would be strange if today's general trend toward mass movements and the flight into the collective had stopped short at the gates of the Church. There is in fact an endless amount of work being done in the Church today, by the clergy, by religious, by lay people. Nobody can be unaware of how much energy and good will is here being brought together, day after day, all over the world. It is more than ever impossible to carry on this tremendous growth of work in the Church without organization, subordination of lower to higher levels, plans and their fulfillment, direction and obedience.

But are we not faced, here again, with the lurking danger of a collectivism that is afraid of responsibility? Do we not, in large things and small, both at the top and at the bottom, more unconsciously than consciously, still find an unfreedom which is crippling free initiative and free action? Do we not very often find hidden here a flight from personal responsibility disguising itself as loyalty to the Church, a timid lack of self-reliance pretending to be subordination, a misplaced waiting for ecclesiastical direction masked as obedience? What we need today is *genuine Christian* obedience. The Church cannot do without this obedience, which is an expression of service in love: ". . . you have been called unto freedom" says St. Paul, but adds at once: "only make not freedom an occasion to the flesh, but by charity serve one another" (Gal. 5, 13).

Obedience in love, which is by that very fact obedience in freedom, does not make men in the Church into what Paul warns us against: "Slaves of men" (1 Cor. 7, 23). The obedience of a free Christian can never be a blind obedience. This century has given us sufficient demonstration of where blind obedience leads. In his very obedience the Christian in the

Church retains his full free responsibility, which he cannot transfer to anyone, to anyone at all.

It follows clearly that obedience in the Church is binding not only on the subordinate but on the superior as well. The latter has the duty, in all the orders he gives, of respecting the freedom of the subordinate. The principle of a totalitarian system, such as violates human freedom, is "Freedom as far as is necessary, constraint as far as is possible." The principle of order in the Catholic Church is the reverse—"Freedom as far as is possible, constraint as far as is necessary": the maximum freedom with the minimum constraint.

This is simply another way of formulating the principle of subsidiarity developed by Pius XI in his encyclical *Quadragesimo Anno*, of which Pius XII said explicitly that it applied, without prejudice to her hierarchical order, to the Church herself. What the individual Christian can do out of his own resources should not be done by the community, or a superior authority. The latter should act only in a subsidiary, supporting way. So also has Vatican II stated:

> For the rest, the usages of society are to be the usages of freedom in their full range: that is, the freedom of man is to be respected as far as possible and is not to be curtailed except when and insofar as necessary.*

Behind the principle of subsidiarity stands the fundamental New Testament truth that it is not only in the superior but also in the subordinate, not only in those who bear office but also in the laity, in short, in *all* Christians, that the Spirit of God, the Spirit of freedom, is at work. If the man who bears office in the Church has confidence in the workings of the

* Second Vatican Council's *Declaration on Religious Liberty*, 7.

Spirit in each individual believer, then he is proof against the
unfreedom of that responsibility-complex which surrounds all
the action and inaction of individual believers with such an
array of safeguards that the joyous freedom of faith is oppressed, the initiative of love is crippled, and the Spirit is
extinguished.

If, on the other hand, the individual believer in the Church
has confidence in the workings of the Spirit in those who bear
office, he is proof against the unfreedom of that anti-clerical
feeling which sees unwarrantable paternalism and will to
power in every action and inaction of the man in office. Thus
confidence in the workings of the Spirit gives true freedom
to each and every member of the Church, and this overcomes
that evil which has done so much harm and hindered so much
good in the modern Church: namely, fear, everyone's fear of
everyone else, and the insincerity and inactivity that go with it.

What sort of Christian, then, does the present situation
call for? Not one who is fear-ridden and insecure, inhibited
and ossified, prim and plaintive, fanatical and filled with resentment, but a Christian who is courageous and self-reliant,
big in ideas and in heart, dynamic and vital, open and joyful.
All this is given by Christian freedom: generosity, tolerance,
balance, serenity, naturalness, humor, individuality, strength,
self-reliance, courage to think and to decide, to hope, and be
joyful.

What vast possibilities are opened up by freedom in the
Church! What possibilities, in particular, in the ecumenical
movement. For we may be sure of this: the more the Catholic
Church makes freedom a reality within her, freedom of
thought, of speech, of writing and of action, the more this
freedom in order of hers will represent an advance towards the

Christians separated from her, who are seeking for order in freedom.

This realization of freedom within the Catholic Church will mean ecumenical encounter more especially if it is understood not only as freedom of individual Christians but also as freedom of individual local Churches. This is an old and justified desire especially of our Orthodox brethren. By "the Church" we understand not only the universal Church. It is just as much the original sense that the individual local Churches are the Church: the Churches of Corinth, Ephesus and Rome; the Churches of Italy, Switzerland, England and the United States; the Churches of Europe, America, Africa and Asia. The Second Vatican Council has once more, in a new way, taken real account of the necessary multiplicity of individual Churches.

Unity, not uniformity; *unitas*, not *uniformitas*; a center, not centralism, is what is called for in the Catholic Church today. The Churches of individual countries and continents are again to have more possibilities for the solution of their own particular problems, worries and tasks; more independence; more freedom. This too would be an application of the principle of subsidiarity.

Freedom first of all in the *liturgy*: One God, one Lord, one Baptism, one Eucharist—but different rites, different languages, different peoples, different communities, different forms of devotion, different styles of art, different prayers, chants, vestments.

Freedom, secondly, in *Canon Law*: One God, one Lord, one Church, one leadership—but different forms of Church order, different orders of law, different nations, traditions, systems of administration, different customs.

Freedom, thirdly, in *theology*: One God, one Lord, one Gospel, one faith—but different theologies, systems, styles of thought, different conceptual apparatus and terminologies, different trends, schools, traditions, different universities, different theologians.

In all this, what holds good is freedom in order and order in freedom. In all this, what holds good is that saying that John XXIII never tired of repeating: *In necessariis unitas, in dubiis libertas, in omnibus autem caritas* (In necessary things unity, in doubtful things freedom, but in everything love).

When, in recent centuries, has the world had such great anxieties and problems as it has today? When, in recent centuries, has the Church, has Christianity had such great opportunities as it has today? Only a free Church, the Church as the free community of the free sons and daughters of God, is capable of fulfilling these chances. Freedom in the Church is not a theory. Freedom in the Church is a reality. Freedom in the Church is a challenge. How much freedom shall be made real in the Church depends on you, on me, on all of us.

3 THE FREEDOM OF THEOLOGY

The truth will make you free!
Jn. 8, 32

In necessary things unity,
in doubtful things freedom,
but in everything love.
St. Augustine

Does a theology of freedom not include and presuppose the freedom of theology? Now that the Second Vatican Council has made so unmistakably clear the fundamental importance of good theology, and of free theology, for the renewal of the Church, for the ecumenical dialogue with other Christians and with Jews, and for promotion of a better understanding on our part of the modern world, we must necessarily search for the meaning of this freedom which Christ has brought to us; what we mean in *theology* by the glorious freedom of the children of God.

We may take for granted that *freedom* is an opportunity for determination as opposed to a dependence on the strength and power of others. Freedom in theology too should not be understood in a negative sense, such as "being free *from* something," but also and pre-eminently as "being free *for* something." Freedom in theology especially should be *intellectual* freedom: freedom of the intellect, of the mind, and at the same time freedom of the intellectuals, in the case of the theologians. I understand, then, the freedom of theology as a manifestation and function of the freedom of the *Church*:

the Church as the freely established community of human beings who believe and love, who have been liberated into a new life, by God's grace in Christ, liberated from the letter of the law, from sin, from death. Since the Church wants to be the dwelling place of freedom, the theology of the Church must also be free. What, actually, is the positive meaning of this freedom which is at once a gift and a task?

Who Represents the Church?

"But with whom are we to discuss these problems of freedom? Who is qualified to be our partner in discussion? Is there anyone at all who really represents, for example, the Protestant Church?" In the days when Catholic and ecumenical theology were two separate things, Catholic theologians used often to pose this kind of question, in the hope of thus dispensing themselves from participation in Catholic-Protestant dialogue. But when such queries are not used as cover for laziness, but put up for serious consideration, they raise a question of the utmost importance with reference both to the Church and to the attitude of the individual theologian. First of all, they put their finger on the crucial wound in Protestant theology. Its divided and mutually contradictory state, which often strikes us as nothing short of chaotic, is a denial of order and unity in the Church to which it belongs; but at the same time it is a denial of the freedom under whose banner it ranged itself in days gone by and still ranges itself today. But at the same time this provokes a rejoinder from the Protestant side which puts its finger on the weakness in Catholic theology. Its restricted and uniform character, which often strikes Protestants as forced and empty, is a denial of the freedom and catholicity of the Catholic Church; but at the same time it is a denial of that very order which is set out to champion in days gone by and still champions today.

Now, it is true that there is no overlooking the fact that the situation has greatly altered, on both sides, in the course of the last few decades. Not only has "Catholica [or "Protestantica"] non leguntur" practically no further application today. In addition to this, a great change has taken place both in Protestant and in Catholic theology, in comparison with, say, the period before the First World War. On the Protestant side, the breakdown of dialectical theology has been followed by a new insistence on taking seriously the Word of God and the decisive statements of faith in the preaching of the New Testament; this is something which today unites, in a new way, schools as different as those of Barth, Bultmann and the orthodox Lutherans, in a common anti-liberal front, and is at the same time conferring a growing theological coherence on the World Council of Churches. On the other hand, in the Catholic world a renewal of the whole of theology has been going on since the First World War, and even more since the second; a renewal which differs from the neo-scholastic restoration of the last century by its growing concentration on Scripture and on the theology of the early Church. This has given Catholic theology a new vitality, manifested in an increase of breadth, dynamism, complexity and capacity for interior tension in theological positions. This has not gone unnoticed outside the Catholic Church. It is normal today to speak of different theological "wings," "camps" and "schools"; people are better at distinguishing between the theologies of different regions, territories and universities; they recognize different types of theologian, etc. And Catholic theologians are realizing, not without a certain amusement, that today they are being set the same question that they have so often set their Protestant colleagues: "Who really represents the Catholic Church?" Progressives or conservatives? Northerners or Southerners? Germans or Romans, Spaniards or French? The Pontifical Lateran University or the Pontifical Biblical Institute? Which dogmatic theologian? Which exegete?

There is no mistaking the fact today of a new awakening in Catholic theology, characterized by a new freedom—an awakening which has been in preparation for decades, and to which the Second Vatican Council has given powerful encouragement. But it is equally unmistakable that this awakening, with its new freedom, has no desire to serve the whims of individuals, but only freedom within order. Any Protestant theologian who wants to compare the present theological movement to that Modernism which provoked such sharply repressive measures from the Church's teaching authority before the First World War should not let the indisputable similarity in the problems being raised lead him to overlook the crucial difference: that all the leading Catholic theologians today earnestly desire to be truly representative of the Church; they want to have the Church behind them in their theology; they want to do theology *for* the free Church and *in* the free Church.

A free theology, then, is free in two ways: first, it is free *for* the Church. This means it is at once scientific in character and pastoral in orientation. Secondly, it is a free theology *in* the Church. This means it is at once critical in outlook and deeply rooted in the Church.

A Free Theology For the Church

The reforms proposed by Modernism, fired as it was with the nineteenth century's enthusiasm over progress in science, and especially in historical research, were primarily scientific and literary in orientation. The theological renewal that is taking place today, stimulated and sustained as it is by the biblical, liturgical, pastoral, missionary and ecumenical renewals, is emphatically *pastoral* in orientation. Its desire is to be a theology *for* the Church. The leading theologians in it are not out for a purely intellectual debate with the modern world and modern science; it is not, for them, simply a matter of self-sufficient intellectual curiosity, of scientific progress and the extension of our philosophical, historical, exegetical and theological knowledge for its own sake.

Though necessarily in a very indirect way (theology neither can be nor aims at being a substitute for preaching), it is rather a matter of service of our neighbor, whether near at hand or afar off; of a perpetual renewal of the Church and her preaching, a better service by the Church of the world and of men in this present age. Thus, while appreciating the limits of the science of theology, they reject that all-too-widespread dichotomy between theology and spirituality which could not but lead on the one hand to a stiff, tedious type of scholasticism, divorced from life, and on the other to a sentimental, introspective, insubstantial kind of pietism. For these theologians, theology and spirituality, science and preaching, dogma and pastoral care, thought and prayer all belong together, distinctions and autonomies notwithstanding. The most important thing about this is not that they find time, along with their scientific research work, to do writing of direct service to spirituality and pastoral practice. It is rather that their scientific writing itself is done not for its own sake, not in the service of some theological "art for art's sake," but in that of the preaching of the Gospel, of the Church as the community of those who hear and believe. It is a theology which aims wholly at serving God the Lord and his Word;

which serves men precisely because it serves God and is thus able to serve the Church, the people who are summoned and called by God; it is a theology *for* the Church.

But precisely because the aim of these theologians is to do theology for the Church, precisely because they wish to serve the Church's preaching and pastoral work, they are convinced that theology with a pastoral orientation cannot be done with facile, unexacting techniques but demands serious scientific research; it must be a seriously scholarly theology. This is the only way for theology to be of real service to the Church. Slack parrot-repetitions of inherited formulas do not deserve the name of theology. Uncritical acceptance of highly problematical concepts; unverified repetition of received opinions on *adversarii*; mere rearrangement and rehashing instead of thoroughgoing rethinking of traditional theses; naïve reiteration of scriptural "proofs" without regard to the results of modern exegesis; dismissal of difficulties presented by the history of the Church and of theology against the opinions one has adopted, by merely making a few *a priori* distinctions in the course of the *responsa ad difficultates*—none of this can be of any service either to the Church's preaching or to her pastoral work. On the contrary, it all constitutes one of the reasons why our preaching and catechesis, our attempts to help and console, our counselling and our answers to inquirers, are often so superficial, inadequate, sentimental and moralistic.

No doubt the trouble often is that those who preach the message have the idea that they have done their theology, once for all and to last a lifetime, once their student years are over. They fail to realize that even a *doctor theologiae* has to keep on being a *studens theologiae*: that indeed it is precisely the man who preaches *sana doctrina* who is under an obligation to find out continually whether, in the course

of progress or regress—of time, of the Church, of theology,
exegesis, history or dogmatics—his doctrine is still *doctrina
sana*. The student of theology who sees the period of his
studium simply as a necessary transition stage, which, happily,
takes only a few short years to get through, and who then,
as preacher, catechist and pastor, fails to keep, so far as possible, abreast of theology, is a man who has never understood
what theology really is and really aims at. Of course, what is
lacking in our priests today, overloaded as they are with work,
is often not goodwill but quite simply time. But this is where
it becomes urgently necessary to seek relief, and work out
how time and energy could be saved. A rather better distribution of priests, rather less club work, less bureaucracy, less
school teaching (lay catechists needed!) might provide the
time for that strictly necessary study and development of
theology which would be of such benefit to preaching and to
pastoral work generally. In any case, it is as true today as
ever that there can be no teaching Church that is not constantly and continually a learning Church; no *ecclesia docens*
that does not have to be continually an *ecclesia audiens,
discens, studens*.

But there is no doubt that the trouble often is that the
professional *doctores theologiae* have failed to convey to their
pupils, during their student years, the realization that the
usefulness and necessity of the study of theology is not confined to the training period of the man who has to preach,
but extends throughout his whole life. Not only students,
but professional doctors of theology, too, can fail to take
their task seriously enough. Thoughtless parrotting of the
latest thing is no more worthy of the name of theology than
lazy parrotting of established formulas. Without intensive
scientific labor, neither biblical nor historical nor systematic

nor practical theology will be able to do its work properly and forge ahead.

The modern Church needs good *exegesis*; exploration, at once humble and alert, perceptively attentive and critically intelligent, of that original and, for that very reason, unique and uniquely binding, testimony to God's saving word and saving work proclaimed to us in the Old and New Testaments. What is needed today is an exegesis that does not dodge problems, either from the fear that means lack of faith or the "tact" that is mere time-serving, but grapples with them boldly, purposefully and concretely; an exegesis that does not explain away the multifariously human and fragmentary character of the biblical witnesses, but perceives the Word of God precisely in that human and fragmentary character; which does not slide into unhistorical harmonization of texts nor, on the other hand, delight in hypercritical dissociation of them; which is neither a prop for lazy-minded, hidebound, unbiblical "orthodoxy," nor leads to scepticism (sometimes marked by a sense of superiority, sometimes merely resigned to itself, but always involving the abandonment of hope); an exegesis in which what is derivative is distinguished from what is original, but which is nevertheless capable of hearing the one Word uttered by all the various witnesses.

The modern Church needs good *history*; history of the Church, history of dogma, history of theology: an exploration, at once well focused and intelligently interpretative, of the history of the Church in all the aspects of her life, in her confessions of faith, her dogmas, her doctrine, her theology. What is needed today is a history of the Church, of dogma, of theology, which, in the first place, always and everywhere does full justice to the facts, neither whitewashing the shadows for the sake of naïve apologetics nor peevishly blackening the

lights; which is neither triumphalist, glorifying everything
whatsoever that has ever been done or said or taught in the
Church, nor cynical, equally ready to disqualify it; which takes
note *both* of construction *and* of demolition, *both* of decadence *and* of renewal, of the transitory within the permanent and the permanent within the transitory, and which remains calm and cool about it while not ceasing to be deeply
involved in it; which is quick and clear-sighted in tracing both
connections and contradictions within the life, activity and
teaching of the Church; which neither sets forth a series of
unmeaning facts nor imposes a preconceived system on them
nor twists the facts of Church history, on the subject of popes
or councils or dogma, for the sake of a dogmatic principle, but
on the contrary practices irreproachable impartiality and the
openness of real love by giving everything whatsoever the place
that belongs to it; and which, nevertheless, does not set itself
up as judge over all earthly things but seeks to serve the
Church by measuring everything, ultimately, against the
original message and image of the Church, since only thus
can it, by giving the teaching of the past, point out in the
present the road into the future.

The modern Church needs good *systematic* theology; an
exploration of God's revelation in all its coherence and fullness of meaning, an exploration which both humbly acknowl-
edges its own ignorance and obediently seeks its knowledge in
the Word of God. What is needed today is a systematic
theology (fundamental theology, dogmatics, ethics) which
does not seek out minute peripheral problems for itself but
accepts the great questions, and answers, presented to it by
the Word of God in the human words of the Scriptures;
which does not take as its standard of importance or unim-
portance (still less of rightness or wrongness) some list of

theses which has come about through the somewhat chance processes of history, but derives the perspectives which it is to throw into relief, the dimensions it is to observe, the stresses it is to lay, and the proportions according to which it is to build, from the Word of God in the Scriptures, as being the primary source and norm of Christian theology; which does not let itself be imprisoned within any philosophy (not even the best) or any *Weltanschauung* (not even the most up-to-date), nor try, on the other hand, to restrict the Word of God and foolishly enclose it within a "closed system," however ingenious; but works serviceably away at constructing a system which it modestly refrains from closing—which, indeed, it gratefully holds always wide open toward the ever greater dimension of God's Word. A theology which does not treat Scripture as a quarry from which to build its own free-floating constructions, which does not put on dogmatic blinkers and pick its way past the results of modern exegesis—uncomfortable as these may often be, though at the same time full of hopeful things—but works shoulder to shoulder with this sister science (which, we may hope, is equally aware of the necessity for cooperation between them) in the service of the one same divine revelation; which, again, does not look on the history of the Church, of dogma and of theology, as a dangerous and deceptively surreptitious enemy, to be confined, so far as possible, to utterances in support of the *doctrina* "*communis*," but which respects facts, takes them seriously and makes them theologically fruitful even when they do not fit in with some thesis or dogma or practice; which, God's revelation itself having entered into history, and the Church's dogma being itself an historical thing, does not tear this unity asunder into a *methodus dogmatica* and a *methodus historica*, reducing history to theological impotence and dogmatics to schematic unreality, but, precisely by dint of being good Christian dogmatics (and not an abstract philosophy of religion) is radically historical in thought and procedure; which thus does not make an artificial separation between doctrine and life, knowing and doing, theory and practice; which holds no brief for, on the one hand, impractical intellectualist dogmatizing, divorced from life, nor, on the other, uninspiring, casuistical, pragmatic moralizing, but which works from the conviction that God's gracious Word is always, at the same time, a word of command making its claim and its demand upon man—dogmatics and ethics in one, or ethics in subordination to dogmatics; which, finally, in all its ways and at every step, is always humbly and practically conscious that it is still seeing only in a glass darkly; that it can still speak only imperfectly, obscurely and partially, and indeed often only stammer and stutter; but which, in all its ways and at every step, is, equally, sustained ever anew by the liberating hope that it will at last, by no effort of its own, be given from above, in grace, that perfect knowledge which is face to face.

The modern Church, finally, needs good *practical* theology; an exploration, at once in touch with our times and critical of them, into the forms which the Church's activity must take in her preaching of the Gospel, her administration of the sacraments, her pastoral work, so that they shall be both true to themselves and adapted to the age. What is called for today is pastoral theology which is not choked with psychology, sociology and pedagogy, does not go to seed over peripheral matters and degenerate into pastoral techniques and tactics without theological content; which, while fully orientated toward the world as it is in this age, is not limited to a pragmatic outlook but holds fast to the Gospel which the Church is there to serve in every area of her pastoral work. What are called for are catechetics and homiletics which are neither primarily interested in method, such as the use of standardized teaching aids, nor bent on merely intellectualist or moralist transmission of knowledge, but which are kerygmatic in orientation, constantly coming back to the Word of God as their center in the proclamation of the Word, in teaching and instruction, in the service of faith. What is called for is a study of the Liturgy which does not indulge in rubricism, ritualism, aestheticism and historicism but, aware both of the Scriptures and of historical development, works at disclosing the real meaning of the whole Liturgy in all its various forms, with a view to active participation in it. What is called for is a study of canon law which does not turn historical developments into absolutes and make a mystique of mere human law, but which takes a healthily historical, demythologizing approach and measures all canons, subsections, decrees and *monita*—as a Christian theological science should, being taught by exegesis and dogmatics—by the standard of the New Testament message itself; which does not tyrannize over men with legalism, formalism and rigorism but acts as the representative of order in freedom, so as to protect in all things the freedom of the children of God.

It is easy to present biblical, historical, systematic and practical theology with such demands. What is difficult is to carry them out; and today—in a world passing through an unprecedented crisis in its spiritual history—more than ever. Theologians who are not engaged in cultivating theories in theological hothouses but out in front amid the harsh winds of intellectual debate are, indeed, particularly apt to be aware of this. They know that today a good systematic theologian has got to be, at least on a limited scale, a good exegete, historian and practical theologian as well, and that, *mutatis mutandis*, this applies to the exegete, historian and practical theologian, too. The present pastoral orientation of theology, with its desire not to talk past men but *to* talk *to* them, does most certainly call for extremely strenuous efforts on all fronts. But there is one absolute requirement in all theology: something that would not need stating, being so entirely obvious to any theologian, if it were not that only too often it is almost in danger of suffocating under the time-serving hypocrisy of "saying the acceptable thing" and the fear of possible repressive measures. The absolute requirement of any theology done *for* the Church, any theology that is at once genuinely pastoral and radically free, is a passionate love of truth.

A Free Theology In the Church

The reforming efforts of the Modernists were made under the influence of nineteenth-century theological liberalism, which for various reasons, not all on its side, was incapable of reaching a right relationship with the Church. Today's theological renewal, with the various experiences behind it, both positive and negative, which it has undergone since the two world wars, is certainly not clericalist, but it does bear a wholly and entirely *ecclesial* stamp. Its desire is to be a theology *in* the Church. Its leading theologians do not take up a sceptical or resigned attitude on the periphery of the Church's life; their position is one of total conviction, right in the center of the Church. They have no desire to be some species of free-floating thinkers, historians, or dealers in speculative ideas, belonging nowhere and hence bound to nobody. What point would there be in their existence as theologians, without the

Church? They want to do their theology not only *for* her but also *in* her. They are well aware that the subject-matter on which they work is not something they have discovered but something they have received. That God's Word has not been uttered to them directly, through some inner illumination (they are not pseudo-mystics), or in a book fallen from heaven (they are not bibliolaters). That, on the contrary, it has come to them by the testimony, tradition and proclamation of the great community of believers, witnessing to God's saving acts first in the Old Testament and then, definitively, in Jesus Christ. It was in this community of the believing People of God, first Israel and then the Church, that the Word of God was originally, through the Holy Ghost, perceived and accepted, heard and believed. Right at the beginning, the Church crystallized this original and hence unique witness of faith, filled with the Spirit, in her Scriptures, which cannot be superseded and which set the norm for all time. Right from her beginning, and on through the centuries, the Church continues to be, in her teaching, the bearer of this witness of faith filled with the Spirit.

Hence any theology which desires to appeal, as Christian theology, to that witness of faith, has always got to grow out of the Church as the community of believers, so as to be of service to her and hence to the world. Without the community of believers it loses its context and its goal. (a) It is through the Church, through the *Canon* which she affirmed and delimited through a long-drawn-out testing process, and repeatedly ratified, for good, not for ill, in succeeding centuries, that the individual theologian knows which writings can be treated as the sound, original testimony of the Spirit. History shows that a theologian cannot with impunity despise this selection, this discernment of spirits, which the Church

has made as a product of her belief. (b) It is through the
Church, through her *confessions of faith* and *definitions*,
made as delimitations against heresy in various historical
situations, that the individual theologian is helped in finding
the difficult road of faith between the different varieties of
false belief, superstition and unbelief. History shows that a
theologian cannot with impunity despise the fences and
danger signs which the Church of former ages, in her battle
to defend the one true faith, has set up to distinguish good
from bad interpretations of the message, often in times of
extreme urgency and danger. (c) The Church, with the
theologians of her past, saves the individual theologian the
necessity of starting from scratch, with no experience, within
one narrow perspective and the limits of one short life, and
thus inevitably finding himself retreading useless blind alleys
and overlooking important discoveries. Here, too, history
teaches us that a theologian cannot with impunity despise
the positive and negative experiences of his fathers and
brothers in theology: those teachers who are his elder and
more experienced fellow pupils in the school of Holy Scripture.

The Word of God is spoken not to this or that individual,
but to this or that individual in the Church. It is not on our
own account and at our own risk, but in communion with
believers past and present, near and far, that we are to perceive
and accept the Word of God, hear it and believe it, get to
know it and penetrate it. Like faith itself, theology, too, is
not simply a private affair but at the same time the affair of
the Church; of the whole Church, insofar as *all* Christians
have a duty to concern themselves with the truth of Christian
witness, and of a few in particular in the Church who, on
behalf of the others, serve Christian witness by devoting them-

selves especially to theological research and teaching so as to be of use to their communities. Only a theologian who has reverently and trustingly listened to the community of the Church to whom God's Word was spoken, only a theologian who does not cut himself off in advance from this common life of hearing the Word, can make any claim to speak to the Church and be heard by her. The theologians who are working today for the renewal of theology are convinced that a theologian can only effectively do theology *for* the Church, and so for the world, if, no matter what the Church's shortcomings and frailties may be, he does not hold loftily aloof from her, does not stand, sceptical and uncommitted, on the sidelines, does not regard himself as raised above the community of believers by membership of some "third denomination" in between Catholics and Protestants, but does his theology right in the middle of the Church, in solidarity with her: theology *for* the Church and *in* the Church.

But precisely because these theologians want to do theology *in the Church*, because, in listening to the Word of God, they want at the same time, in subordination to that Word, to listen to the Church, they are convinced that a theology anchored to the Church cannot be done by using easy, comfortable means, but calls for serious exegetical, historical and systematic criticism and testing; that it has to be a seriously *critical* theology. It is only thus that theology is really of service to the Church. It has to be realistically taken into account that the holy Church of God is a community of men, i.e., a community of sinful and erring men: that though the Church does indeed live by the Word of God, yet, despite all the hearing and obeying done by her members, she is constantly *not* hearing and *not* obeying, too; that along with all her faith there is always false belief, superstition and unbelief as well;

that hence, even in her preaching, teaching and pastoral work, there are tares as well as wheat.

Here, theology has constantly the huge and difficult task of sifting, testing, examining, discerning. This work of discerning (*krinein*), this theological criticism, consists in using all the means of research available to theology as an exegetical, historical, systematic and practical science for the purpose of measuring, testing and correcting the way the Church speaks of God by the standard of the original message in Scripture, the Word of God itself: is all that the Church is doing and saying, in matters great and small, derived, as the Church herself desires it to be, from the Word of God, does it lead back to the Word of God, is it in accord with it? This discerning activity on the part of theology is not directed against authority; what it wants is to help authority in its task with the tools of theological science. Theology cannot take the place of authority in the Church; history proves this. But neither, on the other hand, can authority be a substitute for theology; history proves this, too. Whenever it happens that, in preaching, teaching, pastoral work and the community's and the individual's life of faith, the right emphasis shifts, consciously or unconsciously; whenever, unawares or not, the true proportions get distorted; whenever side issues become main issues and main issues side issues, peripheral things are made central and central things peripheral; whenever truths get obscured or buried or forgotten, and errors or half-truths glossed over and disseminated, then it is time for theology to exercise its function of negative criticism which is at the same time positive and constructive criticism: the continual pointing out, everywhere and with all the means at its disposal, of the main issue, the central point; and, at the same time, the expression, in its fullness, of the whole message.

Do we need to spend any time explaining that this task of criticism and correction is not one that can be carried out once for all, but has to be laboriously performed over and over again? It would be so simple if the deficiencies in what the Church is saying or doing could be effortlessly grasped at first sight, and if what the message of the Old and New Testaments is on a given point in a given situation were equally plain and obvious! But here, as everywhere else, it is not simply a question of what has long been definitively known and hence merely has to be assembled, repeated and restated. We all live in the darkness of faith, and know only enigmatically and partially (1 Cor. 13, 12). It is not by slick, arrogant pouncing, by quick conclusions reached without labor, but by tireless taking of trouble, questioning, seeking, probing, with all the methods of exegesis, history and systematic theology, into Scripture, tradition and the history of the Church, that we arrive, in an ever new historical situation, at a truth that had at first been hidden and is indeed still hidden. There is a lesson to be learned by every generation of theologians from the example of the great Doctors of the Church and their endless labor.

It is precisely at those points where a theologian has to demonstrate his ecclesial character that he has also to demonstrate his character as a searching critic: (a) While holding in all confidence to the *Canon* given him by his Church, he has the right and duty to use all means to investigate, at once humbly and without constraint, how far these writings of the Old and New Testaments witness to the Word of God; how far some of them give their testimony more directly and clearly, others more indirectly and obscurely; how far some of them represent primary testimony, others a derivative one; how far the humanity and weaknesses of the writers have their effect, how far a document is shaped by differences in environment, in character, in theological conception, and again by the faith of the community and by various traditions, etc. (b) While loyally holding to his Church's *confessions of faith* and *definitions*, the theologian has the right and duty to use all means to investigate, at once humbly and without constraint, how far these confessions and definitions bear witness to the Word of God in Scripture; how far they do this more directly, clearly and accurately, or more indirectly, obscurely and approximately; how far some are nearer to and others further from the testimony of the Old and New Testaments; how far they confess and how far they combat; polemicize or expound; affirm or react; declare a judgment or pronounce a condemnation; how far they are spoken in this or that particular direction; how far the humanity and weakness of those who took part in framing them has its effect; how much influence there is from the current historical situation in Church, State, and society; how far there has been an effect from the way questions have been stated because of factors arising from philosophy, psychology or the general cast of thought; how far different languages, different concepts of the world and of man have colored these utterances; how far the traditions of particular nations, schools of theology, universities and orders have been a factor in determining them, etc. (c) While honestly holding fast to his Church's great theologians, the theologian has the right and duty to use all means to investigate, at once humbly and without constraint, how far these theologians, as witnesses to the truth, do testify to the Word of God in Scripture; how far they do this unequivocally or ambiguously, more clearly or less, intelligibly or less intelligibly, emphatically or hesitantly, with or without qualification, loudly or quietly, strongly or weakly;

how far they stand in the great tradition of the Church; how far in them, too, humanity and its weaknesses take their toll; how strongly they are marked by their country and background, those from whom they learned their theology, their individual and collective experiences, their openness or limitations of mind and character, the structure of their thought and their conceptual apparatus; how far they are preconditioned in various ways—physiologically, psychologically, aesthetically, logically, linguistically, ethnologically, historically, philosophically and religiously, etc.

The Catholic doctrine of *infallibility* is not meant to hinder this serious critical effort on the part of the theologian. It is only meant to safeguard it against becoming so wildly arbitrary that it tumbles over itself and negates itself by cutting away the ground from under its own feet. Catholic theology has been able to learn endless positive things from Protestant theology, in exegesis, history and systematic theology, and will be able to go on doing so. But from the Protestant "doctrinal chaos," as it has been called even on the Protestant side, it seems to Catholic theology that there is only something negative to be learned. In any case, there is a mass of questions imperiously confronting Protestant theology at this point, regarding the relationship of the individual theologian to the whole Church, which show that the question of the Church's infallibility may perhaps not be so easy to dispose of as it has been to a great extent by Protestants in one-sided polemics against the First Vatican Council. Protestant theologians need to ask themselves such questions as these: Is there an essential difference between a formulation of faith made by an individual Christian and theologian, and one made by a Council or the whole Church? What is the ground of this difference? Is there nothing behind it beyond the weight

of superior numbers? Is the authority of a formulation of the
faith by the whole Church, then, merely the sum of the authority of formulations made by individual Christians? Or
has a formulation by the whole Church a new specific quality?
From whence would this specific quality derive? Is it enough
to answer this question by recourse to Holy Scripture, seen as
the ground for the formulation? Can it not happen, in some
circumstances, that the individual Christian appeals to Scripture in support of his own formulation, *against* that of the
whole Church? Does not every Christian appeal, in his fashion,
to Scripture? But then why does even the Reformation
Church hold fast, as against all arbitrary individualism, to the
Apostles' Creed and the definitions of the early Councils?
Whence this certainty that, e.g., the Nicaean *homoousios* has
the backing of Scripture? Has not even this become questionable to many people today? Yet why are people in the Church
so anxious to acknowledge the *homoousios* as being in accordance with Scripture, in spite of its remoteness from
Scripture? Is this not done through confidence in the one
same faith of the one same Church, the Church both of the
New Testament and of Nicaea? But why should this confidence in the one same faith of the one same Church stop
in some particular century, such as the fifth? And does this
not show that it is precisely the right understanding of
Scripture itself which would sometimes be in danger without
the faith of the Church, and even, in some circumstances,
the judgment and definition of the Church? Do not the
heretics constantly appeal, just as the Church does, to one
same Scripture? But how is the Church ever to deal with
heresy if she cannot—precisely in order to safeguard the message of Scripture—pronounce a definitively binding judgment
on whether a particular doctrine is in accordance with Scrip-

ture or not? Was Luther ever able to deal with the subjectivist enthusiasts who appealed, like him, but against him, to the Scriptures? Was the Reformation in general ever able to deal with this kind of enthusiasm and subjectivism in theology? How did Paul and the rest of the Apostolic Church deal with the same kind of thing? Is not the terrible splintering that has taken place in Protestantism a sign that some misjudgment has taken place somewhere? That in that tragic historical situation, when so many good evangelical demands were being made, something else was overlooked which the New Testament itself shows must not be overlooked in this aeon of faith, precisely because of the fragmentary nature of our knowledge and the weakness of men: the necessary unity of the whole Church and her faith, and thus the necessary dependence of the individual theologian on the faith of the whole Church; and, again shown from the New Testament, the necessary function of ecclesiastical authority in the service of the unity of the whole Church and her faith, and hence the necessary dependence of individual theologians on ecclesiastical authority in a common service of the faith of the whole Church?

The very sight of Protestant theology addressing itself to questions like these, seriously and without pre-judging them, will make Catholic theology see itself as summoned to an intensified degree to address itself, with equal seriousness and lack of prejudice, to the questions confronting it from the Protestant side. Catholic theology is called upon to clarify, in a new and more convincing way, how far the Church's creeds and doctrinal statements are *norma normata*, i.e., a norm that is subordinate to Holy Scripture, which is itself the norm for them. But Protestant theology is called upon to clarify in a new and more convincing way how far these creeds and statements are *norma normata*, i.e., a truly binding norm for the whole Church and the individual Christian and theologian. The First Vatican Council laid stress—rightly, we Catholics are convinced—on the *binding* character of the Church's formulations of the faith. But, entangled in its debate with Gallicanism, and never having debated with the serious arguments of Protestant theology, it passed over in silence what we may, basing ourselves on St. Paul, call the *fragmentary* nature of the Church's formulations of the faith. For his words apply to every human utterance, including the solemn utterances of councils and popes: "For we know in part, and we prophesy in part. But when that which is perfect is come, that which is in part shall be done away. . . . We see now through a glass in a dark manner: but then face to face. Now I know in part: but then I shall know even as I am known" (1 Cor. 13, 9, 10, 12). Catholic theology has as yet given no adequate answer to the question of what is implied for it by this imperfect, incomplete, enigmatic, partial, fragmentary character of all our formulations of the faith. (I have tried to make a start in *Structures of the Church*, ch. 8, 3.).* The word "infallible" does not express all this, but obviously it does not deny it. More and better thinking is called for on all this, in exegesis, history and systematic theology. Perhaps there will at last be found some more comprehensive concept that will express, better than the concept "infallible," at once the strictly *binding* character and the profoundly *fragmentary* character of the Church's formulations of the Faith, stating the true and permanent content of both in a comprehensive and balanced way. There is a vast work to be done here by Catholic and Protestant theology.

It emerges clearly from all this that a Catholic theologian

* New York, Nelson, 1964.

who is thinking and working critically is not restricted in his
freedom, but he is protected against arbitrariness by his dependence on the faith of the community of the Church. It
is precisely this fact, that he stands in the midst of the believing community of the Church, that preserves him in *true*
freedom. He is safeguarded against making the results of his
research into absolutes. He is made aware of his own in-
escapable character and limitations, which is very much to
the benefit of his theology. This makes him free for the ever-
surpassing truth of God's Word. It follows from this that the
individual theologian does not try to force the results of his
studies on the community of the Church. He does not want
it to be his doctrine that dominates in the Church any more
than anyone else's. He will on the contrary try to be of service
in the Church by laying the results of his work before the
Church so that she can tell whether or not she can recognize
in them her own belief, the belief of the whole community.
Hence the theologian will seek discussion. He will be ready
to be corrected and refuted. He will not think himself alone
in the truth or equate his words with the Word of God. He
will never on principle confront the Church's belief with
distrust, but, whatever critical scrutiny and argument he may
make, he will always reverently and confidently take as his
starting-point that God's Word has never been without witness in his Church nor ever will be; that it is to her, the Church
as a community, that the Lord's promises were given. Hence
the theologian who is thinking and working critically will
always and everywhere have plenty of grounds for humility.

Given this discreet humility, the result of his free, convinced loyalty to the Church, the theologian does not need
to apologize for speaking the truth and the whole truth.
Truths certainly can often be uncomfortable, unpleasant, un-

welcome, inopportune, and indeed "an offense to pious ears."
A theologian will have the sense and discretion to avoid offense when it is unnecessary. But he will not be afraid of
offense given by the truth. He will allow for being misunderstood, for having those who do not understand sometimes
blustering and calling for condemnations, while the timid take
fright and cannot be immediately reassured. He will avoid
what is avoidable, giving the uncomprehending time to acquire
insight and practice self-criticism, and the timid time for ad-
justment and thought. But he will at the same time not
forget how often theologians have given scandal, evil scandal,
not by speaking but by remaining silent; how often, out of
tenderness for so-called "simple pious people," they have
repelled the educated; how often, in doing this, they have
fatally underestimated the open readiness of these "simple
pious people" for the whole truth, and misused them as an
excuse for their own small-mindedness and cowardice. Nor
will he forget how often theologians have, through their
servility and lack of integrity toward Church authority, done
damage precisely to that authority and so to the whole
Church, by thus themselves depriving theology of its claim
on men's belief. A theologian in the Church does not need to
follow the customs of totalitarian systems by constantly addressing submissive speeches, explicitly or implicitly, to the
authorities (usually, on these occasions, simply called "the
Church," as though he were not also the Church himself).
He does not have to keep protesting that his intentions are
honorable, that he is not out to say anything against the
Church and her faith, that he wants to be loyal to the Church,
that he doesn't want to be destructive but constructive, etc.
He can normally take all this peacefully for granted. Even
harmless forms of toadying, flattery and dissimulation are un-
worthy of a theologian. What are needed from him are

honesty and integrity, fearlessness and steadfastness, intrepidity and determination, courage and dignity. So, theologically humble and unassuming though he should be, he
need never lack a calm theological self-confidence: St. Paul
the theologian can be the model for every theologian here.
The theologian does not have to crouch nervously over his
work, trying to squint in every direction at once; he can
hold his head up and look men in the eye as he performs his
service, under God and his Word, toward the Church, the
community of believers.

Theology for the Church and in the Church, at once pastoral
and scholarly, ecclesial and critical: it can be done only in
freedom, the freedom of the children of God. It is by constantly exposing himself, in the community of believers, to
the freedom of God and his Word that the theologian truly
frees himself for true freedom and becomes truly a free theologian. As a truly free theologian he can serve the community of the free children of God, and can count on his
own freedom being respected and supported by all, everywhere.

Multiplicity in Freedom

Freedom in theology is a necessary condition for multiplicity in theology. Compulsion gives birth to uniformity, nar-
rowness and vacuity; freedom to variety, multiplicity, breadth
and richness. If there were in the Church only one united
theology in the sense of one united party, only one single
theological tendency in the sense of one single theological
party line, this would be a sign not of Catholic freedom but of
uncatholic compulsion. "One Lord, one faith, one baptism"
(Eph. 4, 5)—but *different theologies*.

The faith which is rooted in the unfathomable depths of

God's Word, the superabundantly various and manifold wisdom of God (Eph. 3, 10; cf. 1 Pet. 4, 10), is too rich to be exhausted or contained by any one theology. What contrasts there were in the one early Church between the theologies of Justin and Tertullian; Origen and Cyprian; Athanasius and the Cappadocians; Chrysostom and Augustine; Cyril of Alexandria and Leo I; Gregory I and Maximus the Confessor; Isidore of Seville and John Damascene . . . ! And in the one medieval Church, between the theologies of John Scotus Erigena and Anselm of Canterbury; Abelard and the Victorines; Peter Lombard and Bernard of Clairvaux; Albertus Magnus and Bonaventure; Thomas Aquinas and Duns Scotus; William of Ockham and Tauler, Suso, Ruysbroeck; Gerson and Capreolus; Nicholas of Cusa and Torquemada . . . ! And finally, in the one Church of modern centuries, between the theologies of Cajetan and Erasmus; John Eck and Conterini, Suarez and the Spanish mystics; the Molinists and Thomists; Ripalda and Pascal; Bossuet and Fénelon; Gallicans and Ultramontanes; the Catholic Enlightenment and the Catholic Romantic movement; the nineteenth-century Tübingen school and the neo-scholastics; Newman and the Roman school; and so on! There has never been only one theology in the Catholic Church. There will always be several theologies within the one Church and her one faith.

These various theologies—and this brings us back once more to the question with which we began—have all been *representative* of the Catholic Church insofar as (1) they *desired* to represent her, consciously taking their stand in and for the Church, and (2) the Church whom they desired to represent recognized them as being in fact her own, explicitly or implicitly, formally or tacitly, gave them her protection or at least did not disown them outright. So, too, a theology or a theologian of today represents the Catholic Church so long as he fulfills both these conditions. In this sense *every* Catholic theologian and *every* Catholic theology existing today represents the Catholic Church.

But this means at the same time that no Catholic theologian can say that he *alone* represents the Catholic Church. For in this exclusive sense no theologian and no theology represents the Catholic Church. Every theologian and every theology is limited in a particular personal and historical way. Every theologian works on the basis of particular historical presuppositions, and equally with particular historical objectives. Even if his horizons are wide, he always sees things from one particular point of view. He has his own special ways of knowing and thinking, his own particular conceptual apparatus and terminology, his own particular formulations and solutions of problems, his own particular tradition and background, his own particular theological friends and foes. Thus his particular character and limitations—which can at any time lead him into error—are manifold.

Nor has the Catholic Church ever identified herself outright with any particular theologian or theology. There have indeed been theologies which have so set their stamp upon some period, long or short, of the Church's history that her theology might seem to have been based upon these names among all others. But not even the greatest of them (to say nothing of the lesser ones), notwithstanding all the praise lavished on it for a certain period of the Church's life, has escaped undergoing, sooner or later, within the Church, an assessment of its limitations. Pillars of theology like Origen, Cyril of Alexandria, Thomas Aquinas, Bellarmine, etc., have all been recognized, either during their lifetime or later, as inadequate or onesided in some way, and hence corrected.

None of them has proved himself in the long run as "the way, the truth and the life" for the Church.

It is indeed the greatest of the theologies that have had the humility and wisdom to see the problem of their own theological limitations more clearly than others. It will be valuable here to let Augustine speak at length from his introduction to his great work on the Trinity:

It will not vex me to search further at points where I am hesitant; nor shall I be ashamed to learn at points where I am mistaken. So where the reader is as sure as I am, he can go on with me; where he is hesitant, he can consult me; where he recognizes a mistake in himself, he can rely on me; where he recognizes one in me, he can recall me from it. So let us travel the road of love together, striving toward that of which it is said: Seek ever his countenance! Indeed, I should be glad to arrive at a candid, trustworthy understanding of this sort before God our Lord with all my readers for all my books, but especially for this one on the threefold unity of Father, Son and Holy Ghost, because there is no matter on which error is more dangerous or study more laborious or discovery richer in fruit.

So, if anyone says while reading: That is not well said, I do not understand it: let him blame only my mode of expression, not the faith itself: perhaps the same thing can in fact be said more clearly. Besides, no one has ever spoken in such a way that he could be understood in all things by everybody. So if something in my explanations leaves someone dissatisfied, let him consider whether he understands others who have dealt with the same subjects and questions, so that it is in fact I whom he does not understand. If so, let him put my book aside (or throw it away, if he likes) and spend his time and effort rather on those whom he does understand. But do not let him think that I ought therefore to have kept silent, because I am not able to talk so intelligibly and illuminatingly as those whom he understands. For not all works by all writers come into everyone's hands, and hence it may happen that many who are capable of understanding this work of mine never hear of those other, simpler books, but do at least come across this one. So it is still useful to have the same questions treated at the same time in several books, not from a difference in faith but with a difference in presentation, so that the same thing should reach very many people, some in one form, some in another. But if anyone complains of what I have written as unintelligible, when he really cannot understand any careful and penetrating discussion of these questions at all, then he should be concerned about himself, so as to make progress by thorough study, and not with me, so as to silence me.

But if, on the other hand, someone should say while reading: I quite understand what is meant, but it is not in accord with truth, then let him only hold fast to his opinion and refute mine, if it is possible. If he does it in love and in truth and lets me know of it too (if I am still alive), it is from this above all that I shall gather the richest fruit from my own labors. But if it is not possible so far as I am concerned, it is still my wish and will that he shall impart his knowledge to everyone else whom he can reach. But I do meditate on the Law of the Lord, if not day and night at least at every possible moment, and so that my meditations shall not flow away into forgetfulness I want to catch them with my pen, and hope in God's mercy, that he will let me persevere steadfastly in all those truths of which I am certain. But if there is something that I do not rightly understand, then he himself will instruct me about it, whether through interior suggestions and promptings or through his plain Word, or through brotherly discussion. It is this for which I pray, and I lay this prayer trustingly before him, who will surely keep safe what he has given and grant what he has promised (*De Trinitate*, 1, 2, 4–5).

Thus every theologian and no theologian represents the Catholic Church: he represents her in a *limited* and *particular* way. This does not by any means imply that every Catholic theologian is *equally* representative. Augustine, for example, is more representative of the Church than his contemporary Vincent of Lérins. Not only because he wrote more works and dealt with more problems; not only because he wrote more brilliantly and expounded more convincingly; not only because his knowledge was more extensive and his horizons wider; not only because he—alone, perhaps, among the Latin Fathers—was what is called in modern terms a genius; but because through and in all this he succeeded in giving deeper and more comprehensive expression to the *faith of the Church*.

The greatest theologian of the Latin Church during the first millennium was an African. He, like the greatest theologians of the Greek Church, was not a Roman. And this matters for our problem of the relation of the theologian to the Church insofar as it brings in the typical Catholic tension (even Paul lived and suffered under it) between the *periphery* of the Church (which is not "peripheral") and her *center of unity* (which must be understood not primarily as local, but as personal: it was not Jerusalem or Rome but Peter and his successors who were to be the rock of the one Church). Theology and individual theologians, like other fields, display the difference in psychology and laws of behavior between center and periphery: to put it very schematically, the periphery displays those of the front line, the center those of headquarters. But this differentiation, which often makes itself felt very strongly in the practical life of the Catholic Church, is not to be exaggerated in its importance for theology. It is not of decisive importance for a theologian's representative status whether he is working at the center or on the periphery of the Church. Neither the theologian of the center nor the theologian of the periphery can be representative of the Church in an exclusive sense. Each can speak genuinely and validly for the Church in his own way. In theology as elsewhere, the center and the periphery have each its own kind of strength, which are at the same time its hidden or obvious weaknesses. To be schematic again, we may say that in theology the center is concerned above all for unity and continuity, the periphery for life and progress. The center's love is for measure, rule, harmony and strict order, the periphery's for movement, multiplicity, discussion and vital development. The center concentrates on proclaiming general principles; it sanctions what is new and provides for safety. The periphery demands the application of principles to the concrete situation; it discovers new things, and calls for daring.

But it is vitally necessary that in theology these tendencies in center and periphery should *not* become the exclusive, rooted attitude of either, but that both center and periphery should look at the whole, which is the Church. The center must not harden into vain, unecclesial arrogance and a reactionary state of mind; into centralism and a superfluity of authoritative interventions; into the demand for a formalist, legalist *sacrificium intellectus*. Conversely, the periphery must not dissolve into self-assured, unecclesial presumption and a revolutionary state of mind; into decentralism and a superfluity of unbridled discussion; into the demand for a false freedom which is mere arbitrariness. It is of vital importance that center and periphery should not become isolated from each other in theology; that they should be completely open toward each other, held together in unfettered exchange and dialogue. In this way the theologians of both center and periphery will come to be representative of the Church in a fuller and deeper sense. In this way the center will constantly appear as being in the front line, too, a front that always ultimately runs through the center as well; and the periphery as at the same time the heart of the Church, in which there is no part that can be simply peripheral.

By open interchange and mutual help Paul not only prevented the tension in the Catholic Church of his time, between Jerusalem and the periphery, from growing to breaking-point, but made it, through respect on both sides for Christian freedom, into something fruitful. It is for us through this same mutual respect for freedom in the Church today to preserve this tension between center and periphery, to reduce it, and to make something fruitful of it.

Outsider or Vanguard?

Faced with the fact of a renewal and reform in the Catholic Church and her theology, there is a certain type of outmoded anti-Catholic apologetics (which still exists, like outmoded Catholic apologetics) which has taken tactical refuge in the contention that these movements of theological renewal are a marginal phenomenon in the Church and that the theologians active in them lead a marginal existence in her. The unproved axiom behind this, which is meant to lull to sleep again those Evangelical Christians who have been healthily disquieted by the positive changes taking place in the Catholic Church, runs like this: The Catholic Church just *doesn't* change—not for the better, anyway! On this view, it is hardly possible for the theologians who represent a renewal and reform of the Church and of theology to be anything but deviationists, roughly lumped together with the Modernists under the label "reformist Catholicism," bound, for the most part, to be condemned sooner or later by the Church's teaching authority, and in any case representing only a transitory phenomenon in the history of the Catholic Church. It is thus that apologetes of this sort perpetuate anti-Roman feeling and cut the ground in advance from under any genuine ecumenical encounter with the Catholic Church.

This notion, which, we may rejoice to say, is finding fewer and fewer adherents among Protestants, is false. Only a deficient knowledge of the Catholic Church, or else confessionalistic narrow-mindedness, could ignore the fact that the renewal going on in Catholic life and doctrine is not the affair if a few theological outsiders but of the Church herself. It is certainly true that in our Church we are particularly interested in continuity with the Church of former centuries and have no desire, in doctrine or in life, for an unreliable, weathercock kind of Church; in a good sense, then, the Catholic Church ought to remain the same, insofar as this means remaining the Church of Christ and according to the will of Christ. But for this very reason the Catholic Church is an *ecclesia semper reformanda*, and, as we can gladly and without arrogance affirm, an *ecclesia semper reformans*. So, precisely because the Catholic Church desires to remain the same Church of Christ, she has continually changed herself: in particular, after the decadence of the late Middle Ages and the sounding of the alarm by the Protestant Reformation, she did so first in the reforms of the Catholic restoration and then more than ever in the modern Church as she has been since Leo XIII. I have described this elsewhere.* The enhanced position of Scripture in the preaching, life and teaching of the Catholic Church; the liturgical renewal, with the development of the Catholic Liturgy into a genuine people's Liturgy; the growing sense of the Church as the People of God, and hence of the universal priesthood of the faithful; the improved adaptation of the Church to the different nations and fuller respect for the individuality of the local Church; better understanding of the East-West schism and of the Protestant Reformation as religious challenges and, following this, intensive efforts for ecumenical encounter with Eastern and Evangelical Christians—who, in face of the Second Vatican Council, would now dare to say that all this and so much else in the Church's theology and life are only the concern of a few outsiders and not of the Catholic Church herself? Or if we want to indicate a few specific instances of theological progress (with reference to actual official documents of the Church's teaching authority): Compare the negative attitude of the Council of Trent toward the universal priesthood and the significance of charisms and ministries in the Church with the positive statements in the

* See the author's *The Council, Reform and Reunion* (New York: Sheed and Ward, 1961), esp. Chap. 2–4.

encyclical *Mystici Corporis*; the negative statements of the
Council of Trent on the active share of all the faithful in
the celebration of the eucharistic Liturgy with the positive
ones in *Mediator Dei*; Trent's decisions on the Vulgate with
what is said in the encyclical *Divino afflante Spiritu* and the
replacement of the Vulgate in the official translation of
the Psalms; Trent on the use of the vernacular in the Mass
with current practice in community masses and the reforms
of the Second Vatican Council; the extensive prohibition of
private Bible reading by the laity in the vernacular until well
into the nineteenth century, with the recommendations of
private Bible reading by the popes of this century; the practical rejection of historical and critical methods of exegesis
by the anti-Modernist decrees with the recommendation
of these methods in more recent Church documents; the emphasis still being laid in the nineteenth century on the necessity of having a Papal State with the far-reaching de-politicizing
and growing spiritualization of the papacy in this century;
the rejection of confessional toleration and religious freedom,
even in the last century, with the statements of the bishops
and popes of our day. . . . Who could maintain that all this
is not a matter of the Church herself but only of a few theological outsiders?

But what is true is this: Before there could be progress of
this sort in the Church as a whole, there had to be a few who
went out in front. But there is a decisive difference here
which the anti-Catholic apologetic referred to above prefers
to overlook: the difference between outsiders in theology and
what one may call the theological vanguard. Franz von
Baader, for all his genius as a philosopher and theologian, was
an outsider in the Catholic Church. His contemporary, Johann
Adam Mohler, isolated as he and his friends at Tübingen

might seem against the background of theology as it was being currently taught, proved to be not an outsider but the vanguard.

The outsider works, studies and fights on his own responsibility, so to speak, and at his own risk. Without being particularly concerned about his connection with the main body he sets about constructing a road for himself on its flank— whether because he is a specially daring spirit, or out of disillusionment. Boldly playing a lone hand, he often achieves a breakthrough in some unexpected place and makes discoveries in unexplored territory. If he is a person of stature, the outsider receives admiration; but on the whole he has no following. The Church may perhaps pick up some suggestions and ideas from him, but she does not follow him along the road he has marked out. The theological outsider is only to a very limited extent representative of his Church, though deserving, in his own special individual character, of her respect and honest appreciation.

While the theological outsider works and studies and fights for the Church apart and to one side of her, the theologian of the vanguard does all this with the Church behind him. He cares greatly about his connection with the main body, and however boldly he may press forward he never wants as a theologian to go his own private way, but the Church's way. He is a theological pioneer for the pilgrim People of God on its migration through the darkness and toil of time, not engaged in making a road on which no one can follow him; a trail-blazer, not breaking new ground for the pleasure that he personally takes in research, but on behalf of the whole community of believers; a forerunner and skirmisher, careful not to lose touch with the main body but to maintain intellectual contact with it at all times; not given to marching wildly off in all directions and then, suddenly finding himself on his own, content to be cut off and eliminated, but adapting himself as far as possible, without making material concessions, so as to keep in step with the main body—indeed, even being considerate so far as possible to the slowest-paced section of the rearguard, which in theology is never going to be small in numbers. He has no wish to make his being in advance a form of domination, but only of selfless service; he does not want to play field-marshal: he is simply a scout. While the outsider can only be representative of the Church to a very limited extent, the theologian of the vanguard is so to an especial degree, insofar as he has with him not only the Church's present but her future.

The vanguard of the Church and theology is often small, yet often decisive. After the end of the Middle Ages and the abysmal decadence of the Renaissance, the state of the Catholic Church in Rome looked hopeless. What was it that made possible a recovery from that desperate situation? Fundamentally, the decisive move came from a very few small groups who seemed to be up against both the spirit of the age and, to a great extent, of the Church: obscure Italian fraternities and oratories like the combined clerical and lay "Oratory of Divine Love," and the reformist group that gathered in Venice round the man who was later to be the great Cardinal Contarini. The men in the College of Cardinals who then worked to carry out reform (Contarini, Pole, Fisher, Cervini, del Monte, Morone, Caraffa) had been summoned to it by a pope who himself lagged far behind their ideas for reform and who was personally swayed by the spirit and way of life of the Renaissance; yet under their influence he finally gave approval to Ignatius of Loyola's Society of Jesus, and summoned the Council of Trent. What had been begun by a few

eventually made Church and world history. And so it has
often been since. Neither the social movement with its encyclical *Rerum novarum*, nor the ecclesiological renewal with
Mystici corporis, nor the Biblical renewal with *Divino afflante
Spiritu*, nor the liturgical renewal with *Mediator Dei* would
ever—like so many other things in this century—have been
possible but for those few who, often unrecognized and today
almost forgotten, prepared the way for these ideas, had to
endure bitter misunderstanding and savage attacks from above
and below, but yet, with success still far off, went unresent-
fully on their way and so set the pace for something whose
achievement in all its greatness was to be seen only by the
next generation.

It often takes a long time to settle whether a theologian
is an outsider or a forerunner. In 1277, three years after his
death, Thomas Aquinas was condemned by the bishops of
the two leading universities of Christendom, Paris and Oxford: "the heaviest condemnation of the Middle Ages," says
Van Steenberghen. It brought the free development of theology to a standstill for a considerable period. Who would
have thought that this same Thomas Aquinas, then accused
of Aristotelian modernism, would one day be proposed as the
special model of Catholic theologians? Who would have
thought that this same Thomas Aquinas, accused of *théologie
nouvelle* by the conservative Augustinian theologians of his
day, would be exalted as *doctor communis* by the conservative
theologians of a later day in so exclusive a fashion that the
very popes who had recommended Thomism were obliged to
emphasize that other theological schools besides it did have
right of domicile within the Catholic Church. Aquinas is the
typical example of a theologian who might have looked like
an outsider but was in reality a theological pioneer. He will

always be a model for theologians, as a theologian who knew
how to read the signs of the times; who knew that the old
solutions have to be rethought; who sensed that a new age
posed new problems calling for new answers; who was modern
in the highest degree in accepting the challenge of debate
with the new philosophy and theology dominated by the
influence of Arab Aristotelianism; who was not content with
sterile defense and tired apologetics on behalf of old positions,
but with bold intrepidity opened new doors and trod new
paths in theology; who interpreted Christian tradition anew
through intensive study of sacred Scripture and of contemporary philosophy; who, humble before the Word of God,
never made himself and his own theology a standard of
measurement; who, through the whole of his work in the
theological vanguard, achieved a realization of freedom in
theology to an exceptional degree. Anyone who feels inclined
to take up arms against theological renewal today by appealing to Thomas Aquinas needs to consider whether, had he
lived a few hundred years earlier, he would not have found
himself subscribing to the condemnation of Thomas Aquinas.

A Liberated and Liberating Science

In the final section of the article on "Reformist Catholicism," in that standard Evangelical work, the dictionary *Religion in Geschichte und Gegenwart,* 3rd ed. (Tübingen,
1961), vol. 5, p. 903, we read:

Reformist Catholicism has other norms from ours, so
that all that reformation can mean to it, at most, is the
removal of abuses. Radical return to the Gospel of Jesus
Christ is not necessary for all this "correction of the

Church," and indeed does not lend itself to all this zeal-
ous setting to rights by attention to momentarily deplor-
able conditions in the Church. . . . In the opinion of
Evangelicals, it is not a question of individual reforms
within the Church of Christ, but of the *Church's* being
reformed according to God's Word.

This sets before us the second argument in use by a certain
anti-Catholic apologetic which, I rejoice to say, does not find
too frequent expression in this dictionary. The first argument,
cited above, that the Catholic Church does *not* change, has
already been refuted in this article: "It has rightly been recognized recently that the view (apt indeed to be tacit) that
it is only Protestantism as against Roman Catholicism that
is *ecclesia semper reformanda needs* to be revised or re-inter-
preted. . . . Roman Catholicism is, indeed, a Church of reform. . . ." (p. 902.) But the second argument also falls to
the ground. Why? After all that has been said, we can summarize briefly:

(1) What matters is not who talks loudest about "return
to the Gospel of Jesus Christ" and "reform according to
God's Word," but who acts according to it. It needs to be
said again and again that to bear the name "Reformed" (in
whatever sense—Calvinist, Lutheran, Free Church) puts a
Church in danger of regarding "reform according to the Gospel" as a mere program, or as a task happily carried out once
for all during the Protestant Reformation.

(2) It is indisputable that the movements of Catholic
renewal—biblical, liturgical, theological, pastoral, missionary
—which are briefly noted in this article itself do in fact represent (if often in too unconscious and unplanned a way, yet

for all that in practice quite plainly) a thoroughly energetic "return to the Gospel of Jesus Christ." What the leading theologians in this renewal care about (the article names among others E. Przywara, K. Adam, R. Grosche, O. Karrer, A. Rademacher, Y. Congar, Teilhard de Chardin, J. Lortz), though again perhaps sometimes in too unconscious and unplanned a way, yet again quite plainly in practice, is a reform of theology and of the Church "according to God's Word" (the differences between this and Modernism have already been pointed out).

"Our desire in this assembly is, under the guidance of the Holy Spirit, to seek out how we are to renew ourselves so that we may conform more and more to the Gospel of Christ": Such was the proclamation of the assembled Fathers of the Second Vatican Council in their opening message to the world. Would it not be better to rejoice, on the Protestant as well as on the Catholic side, that the Catholic Church, like the Protestant Church, is striving today—against many difficulties and setbacks, it is true—to renew the Church and theology according to the Gospel of Christ, rather than to try to prove, in defiance of the facts, that the contrary is the case? It is precisely here that our common hope for the present ecumenical movement lies: that we shall be working theologically and practically from *all* sides in a new way for the Gospel of Jesus Christ.

Let us go back to the beginning: Which theology is going *in the long run* to be *representative* of the Church? Which theology is going to prove and establish itself, against all setbacks, as in a special way representative of the Church? Not the one that claims to be specially modern. Nor the one that claims to be specially traditional. But the one that is *backed by the Gospel of Jesus Christ itself*. The one that is founded

not on man's word but on God's; that aims in all its utterances to proclaim not man's wisdom but God's; that theo-
logia, in fact, which speaks of God only insofar as it hears his
Word and responds to his Word, orientated to it and measured by it.

In the Word of God, given by the testimony of men,
theology finds its creative ground and its life. That Word
which God has spoken and still speaks; which is at once his
utterance, his act and his mystery; which proclaims good
news, the *euangelion* of God's gracious saving act in Christ
Jesus, and makes it effective—this Word of God makes theology truly *free*: open to God in service, so as thus to be open
in service to men.

This is a freedom that theology cannot achieve by working
for it, by striving for it, by snatching at it. It can only implore
it. It is a freedom which can only be granted to theology, by
grace, in faith, through the Spirit. "Where the Spirit of the
Lord is, there is freedom" (2 Cor. 3, 17). In this freedom
of the Spirit, theology can be a serious, thankful, honest, confident, unworried, joyful, victorious science. In the freedom
into which Christ has liberated us, in the glorious freedom
of the children of God, theology too can be a liberated and
thus liberating science: in the Church and for the Church,
for the salvation of the world.

4 THE FREEDOM OF RELIGIONS

If the son makes you free,
you will be free indeed!

Jn. 8, 36

The Catholic Church rejects nothing that is
true and holy in these religions. She regards
with sincere reverence those ways of conduct
and of life, those precepts and teachings which,
though differing in many aspects from the ones
she holds and sets forth, nonetheless often re-
flect a ray of that Truth which enlightens all
men.

> *Second Vatican Council's Declaration
> on the Relation of the Church to
> Non-Christian Religions, 2*

Christianity as Minority

In his book *Eastern Religions and Western Thought*, Sarvepalli Radhakrishnan makes use of a story which may well be
taken as characteristic not only of Buddhism and Hinduism
but of many other educated non-Christians in Asia:

> Once upon a time, Buddha relates, a certain king of
> Benares, desiring to divert himself, gathered together a
> number of beggars blind from birth, and offered a prize
> to the one who should give him the best account of an
> elephant. The first beggar who examined the elephant
> chanced to lay hold on a leg, and reported that an ele-
> phant was a tree-trunk; the second, laying hold of the
> tail, declared that an elephant was like a rope; another,
> who seized an ear, insisted that an elephant was like a
> palm-leaf; and so on. The beggars fell to quarrelling with
> one another, and the king was greatly amused. Ordinary
> teachers who have grasped this or that aspect of the truth
> quarrel with one another, while only a Buddha knows the
> whole. In theological discussions we are at best blind beg-

gars fighting with one another. The complete vision is
difficult and the Buddhas are rare. Asoka's dictum represents the Buddhist view. "He who does reverence to his
own sect while disparaging the sects of others wholly
from attachment to his own, with intent to enhance the
splendour of his own sect, in reality, by such conduct
inflicts the severest injury on his own sect."*

It is perhaps an open question whether Radhakrishnan's
tolerance derives chiefly from the Vedanta or rather from
Western idealism and nineteenth-century theological liberalism. The important point for us is precisely that this type of
tolerance is characteristic of a large number of people of *both*
East and West. How many Europeans and Americans are
there who would, in one way or another, subscribe to these
words of Gandhi's: "I believe in the Bible as I believe in the
Gita. I regard all the great faiths of the world as equally true
with my own. It hurts me to see any one of them caricatured
as they are today by their own followers."†
But let us as believing Christians be realistic and not immediately start complaining of "relativism" and "indifferentism." Is it so easy for us to deny the large measure of
breadth and depth that speaks through this view, the generosity and magnanimity, the compassion and human concern,
radically opposed to all the vast mass of religious prejudices
and misunderstandings, religious conflicts, and that real contradiction in terms, "wars of religion"? Does not this view
perhaps rest upon a vision of God that is greater, more exalted, more reverent than the vision of those for whom God

* Sarvepalli Radhakrishnan, *Eastern Religions and Western Thought* (New
York, Oxford U. Press, 1940), pp. 308ff.
† Quoted from Radhakrishnan, *op. cit.*, p. 313.

is allowed to be only the God of one party, one religious party?

Are we not forced to think a little, when we set these Buddhist and Hindu testimonies side by side with a classic testimony of Catholicism, in the explicit form in which it was solemnly proclaimed to the world by Pope Boniface VIII eighteen hundred years after Buddha, and in which it is still to be read today in Denzinger's *Enchiridion*: "We are required by faith to believe and hold that there is one holy Catholic and apostolic Church; we firmly believe it and unreservedly profess it; outside it there is neither salvation nor remission of sins. . . . Further, we declare, say, define and proclaim that to submit to the Roman Pontiff, is, for every human creature, an utter necessity of salvation" (Denzinger, 468f.). Again and again this "Outside the Church no salvation" has been repeated and re-emphasized. But the situation has grown more and more difficult: not only for the Catholic Church, but also for the Protestant Churches, some of which take an even more exclusive stand in regard to the world religions—hence for the whole of Christendom. It is necessary at this point to recall to mind certain facts, all of them only too familiar to us, but the full combined force of which needs to be kept before our eyes if we are to be serious enough in our search for an answer. These, then, are the questions men are asking us today:

Outside the Church no salvation: Can you actually keep on saying this when you look with honesty at the *present time*, and consider that of the more than three billion present inhabitants of the earth only about 950 million are Christians, and that of these only about 584 million are Catholics? That in India only 2.4% are Christians and only 1.2% Catholics, while in China and Japan only about 0.5% are Christians? That even in Europe, both in the great cities and in many rural areas, only a fraction of those calling themselves Christians take any practical part in the Church? What have you to say about this salvation of these millions who live in the *present time* outside the Catholic Church and altogether outside Christianity?

Outside the Church no salvation: Can you keep on saying this when you look without prejudice at the *past*, and consider that the years of humanity's existence before Christ and without Christ are not, as the Bible suggests, five thousand two hundred (a figure which already troubled the minds of the Fathers of the Church) but may amount to six hundred thousand or more; so that the question which the Church Fathers used to ask, "Why did Christ come so late?" has taken on a sharpness of an entirely new kind? What have you to say about the salvation of the countless millions who have lived in the *past* outside the Catholic Church and altogether outside Christianity?

Outside the Church no salvation: Can you keep on saying this when you look realistically at the *future*, and consider that statistics show that numerically the non-Christian nations of Asia and Africa are going to outstrip by far the Christian nations of the West? That merely to preserve the present numerical relationship there would have to be, not the half-million converts to the Catholic Church which there are each year, but six and a half million? That it has been calculated that by the year 2000, China alone may number seventeen hundred million people, four hundred million more than the present population of Europe, the Soviet Union, North and South America, and Africa combined? What have you to say about the innumerable millions and billions who are going to live in the *future* outside the Catholic Church and altogether outside Christianity?

Now, we are all aware of these facts. But do we not need

to come to terms in a new way *theologically* with the fact
that, in face of past, present and future, in face of human
history on *all* continents and in *all* epochs, we, the Catholic
Church and Christendom generally, are clearly a *small, insig-
nificant minority.* Looked at in this way, the problem is by
no means only one for the churches of the missions, but
equally for the churches at home. Yet it remains a special
problem for the missionary churches for this reason: that it
would seem that the age of mass missionary achievements, in
Asia at any rate, is over as far as the foreseeable future is concerned. To get the whole problem clear, we need at this point
to refer to two other aspects of it, both of them again well
known:

1. In our day a period of world history is coming finally
to an end; the one which is called in Europe "the modern
age" and which began four hundred years ago with the discovery of what were to us new continents. The peoples of
Asia and Africa are enthusiastically adopting western science,
technology and industrialization, and thus a world-economy
and a world-civilization are taking shape. But at the same time
something else has become an accomplished fact in a few
years: the age of the political, economic and cultural expan-
sion of the white peoples, of exclusive western domination
of the world, and of all that goes by the name of colonialism,
is over. We all know that the situation of the Christian missions, excessively linked as they have been with that age and
its political, cultural and social system, is not being made any
easier by this change. They are no longer borne along by the
current but have to swim against it. They are being forced in
a new way to justify their work, which is very difficult. And
we can sense that "No salvation outside" is not good enough
an answer. As for our problem, in any case, we have to realize

that today evangelization is directed less and less toward "poor heathens," but rather toward modern men in industrialized states with great and ancient cultures.

2. It is not only politically and socially, not only economically and technologically, that the peoples of Asia and Africa are entering upon a new period of world history, but religiously as well. What many Christians expected has not taken place: the old religions, confronted by European culture and hence by the Christian religion, have not slowly but surely withered away. True, religious indifferentism is growing apace in the countries of Asia and Africa as elsewhere, but the great non-Christian world religions, Hinduism, Buddhism, Mohammedanism, not only are not withering away but are developing with fresh vigor. The four hundred years of the Christian missions were for them—as the Indian writer K. M. Panikkar, for instance, emphasizes in *Asia and Western Dominance**—merely a transition stage during a period when the peoples of Asia were politically and culturally weak. In their eyes, the age of the Christian missions is, as a whole, over and done with. The non-Christian world religions have to a great extent passed over from the defensive to the offensive. Along with the rest of the great and ancient history of its peoples, Asia is reflecting on the great tradition of its ancient religions. In Hinduism, indeed, this process of reflection has long been in operation, precisely because of the pressure of Christianity. On the one hand this renaissance of the world religions leads to an assimilation of the heritage of western thought (as witness Radhakrishnan), and, on the other, to the development of a not inconsiderable missionary drive, threatening a reversal on the religious front. We become all the more aware that "no salvation outside" is not a

* New York, Hillary, 1959.

good enough answer in this new, direct competition with the great world religions. For the purposes of our problem we need to realize that the theological question facing us today is not merely that of the individual person outside the Church and Christianity but of these *religions themselves* outside the Church and Christianity.

An answer of some sort must be given. Is the minority to be prohibited from inquiring about the fate of the majority: is it not rather obliged to do so? The questions arising are so urgent, for the churches both at home and in the missions, that we are absolutely required to face the problem. We cannot, as theologians sometimes do, solve it by recourse to a "dialectical theology" employing an *a priori*, negative, polemical concept of "religion": the idea that in the world religions "religion" means simply a projection of psychological need and an attempt at self-help, that it is a work of human autonomy, a taking care of oneself and asserting of oneself in the face of God, that it is an expression of fear and falsehood and, ultimately, of unbelief and godlessness. It is quite illegitimate for Christians to assume or assert this idea as self-evident; it would need to be established, with all the necessary distinctions and nuances, as true of the present situation. But as soon as we try to do this, we come up against the real ambivalence in the term "religion," which prevents any concept of it from being purely negative.

Nor can we, faced with all the questions arising from the mass of mankind outside Christianity, content ourselves with a polite theological "ignoramus." The European finds it only too easy to compensate for his lack of knowledge about world religions by passing arrogant judgment on that which he does not know. If we cannot give an adequate answer to these questions we must not be surprised if the men of today either content themselves with enlightened indifferentism, like Less-ing with his fable of the three rings, each claimed as genuine and none in fact the father's real ring, or else follow Voltaire in pouring scorn on the arrogance of "salvation monopolists." After two thousand years of Christian history and missionary effort, the plurality of religions still persists. This, even more than the distressing plurality of the various Christian confessions, makes questionable a claim to be absolute on the part of that faith which, more than, and in a different sense from, any other world religion, claims the support of a uniquely valid revelation of God. A theologian has got to inquire seriously whether, to someone whose Christianity is not a matter of mere repetition but of reflection, the revelation of Christ does not have something positive to say on these questions concerning the salvation of pagans (that is, the "unevangelized"), ancient and modern.

We shall in the first instance try to reach toward an answer by the closer examination of the axiom "No salvation outside." This introduces us to what may be called an ecclesiocentric view of the problem. We shall see later on that another view of it is also possible.

Outside the Church No Salvation?

The axiom "extra Ecclesiam nulla salus" goes back to the image of the Ark of Noah, used in 1 Pet. 3:20 to portray salvation through baptism. But we note that while this text does indeed state positively that there is "salvation inside the ark," it makes no simple assertion that there is "no salvation outside the ark." Rather, the text says that Christ, who "died for sins once for all, the righteous for the unrighteous, that he might bring us to God" (3:18), preached the good news after his death to "the spirits" (the fallen angels or the godless generation of the time of the flood, or both) "who formerly did not obey" (3:19–20), and hence were not inside the ark. The text would then mean that even the worst of sinners, even after this life, is not excluded from Christ's call to salvation. So what we have here is in fact an assertion of "salvation outside the ark," with the presupposition of "no salvation outside *Christ*."*

The axiom itself began to be worked out by Ignatius of Antioch, Irenaeus, Clement of Alexandria and others, receiving from Origen its first complete formulation, now cast in negative terms: Outside this house, that is, the Church, no one is saved (*In Jesu nave* 3, 5, *PG* 12, 841). The axiom was applied by Cyprian with fully consistent juridical exclusiveness (*De unitate Ecclesiae* 6: CSEL III/1, 214f.). And here at once we encounter something that has been constantly verified on later occasions: whenever this axiom in its *negative* formulation has been taken in the precise literal sense of the words, it has led to heresy. Thus Cyprian—consistently, as it might surely seem—concluded from it that baptism administered by heretics outside the Church was invalid, and that martyrdom outside the Church was valueless. Cyprian's position was rejected by the Church. Although, unlike Cyprian, Augustine distinguishes between more and less grave cases of heresy, he too could see no possibility of salvation even for the less grave cases. The strict literal sense in which the axiom was taken is shown in this sentence from Augustine's disciple, Fulgentius of Ruspe: "Hold fast as most certain and have no manner of doubt that not only all heathens but also all Jews and all heretics and schismatics who die outside this present Catholic Church will go into that everlasting fire which was prepared for the devil and his angels."

Medieval scholasticism is entirely in line with Augustine.

* For the history of the axiom, see the references in my essay in *Festschrift G. C. Berkouwer*, 1965.

Here again the axiom led to errors which have since been rejected by the Church, as for instance that priests separated from the Catholic Church lose the power to consecrate. And the very Pope who produced the most rigid formulation of "Outside the papal Church no salvation" was the one who brought the papacy to the very brink of disaster (the taking prisoner of Boniface VIII and the Great Western Schism with three Popes all excommunicating each other); the rigorous doctrine of the bull *Unam Sanctam* was not maintained by subsequent popes.

But what was needed to effect a break-through was the tremendous historical event of the discovery of whole new continents with civilized and morally good inhabitants. Now it was not merely *known* that there were lands and peoples outside the Church (this fact was *known* in the Middle Ages); now it became unavoidable to take a positive *interest* in them. After the assimilation of this lesson of history it was now taught not only by theologians like Bellarmine and Suarez but by the Council of Trent as well (Denzinger, 796) that baptism could be received not only, as by Christians, *in re* (baptism of water), but also *in voto* (baptism of desire). Against the rigorism of the Jansenists, the proposition was condemned that "Outside the Church there is no grace" (Denzinger, 1379). Finally, Pius IX so interpreted the meaning of "outside"—in reference not only to unbaptized pagans, but also to Christians separated, as they had now been for many long years, from the Catholic Church—that he was able at the same time to affirm explicitly: ". . . it must equally be held as certain that those who labor under ignorance of the true religion, if this ignorance be invincible, are not held guilty in this respect in the Lord's eyes. But now, who would be so arrogant as to lay down the limits of such ignorance, considering the nature and variety of peoples, religions, intel-

ligence and so many other things?" (Denzinger, 1647). And
when the encyclical *Mystici Corporis* once more gave a somewhat rigorous formulation of the axiom, and Fr. Feeney with
a group of Catholics in Boston tried to take the words of the
encyclical quite literally, declaring, like the early Fathers of
the Church, that everyone outside the Catholic Church was
damned, the Holy Office had to intervene, to protest against
this statement* and finally, by excommunication, to declare
extra Ecclesiam a person who stated that no one could be
saved outside the Church. Fr. Feeney has so far not made his
submission.

Now, what had in fact been happening here, in these interpretations extending from Trent to Pius XII? What had in
fact been done was to state perfectly clearly, even while
formally maintaining the "no salvation outside" axiom, that
there *is* salvation even outside the Church, outside the visible
Catholic Church (which is how the word had always been
understood in Catholic tradition). But this ambiguous mode
of expression has been a source of confusion to a great many
Catholics. Today they do not know how they are supposed
to take the statement that there is "no salvation outside the
Church," since on the one hand they have to say that outside
the Church there is *no* salvation, and on the other they are
supposed to admit that outside the Church there *is* salvation.
Is there salvation outside the Church or not? An honest answer to the question has to be "Yes" or "No," not "Yes and
No."

In order to arrive at a clarification, which needs to be something more than a clarification of idiom and linguistic usage,
I should like to contribute a few propositions to the discussion by which even those who are not specialists in theology

* See the Letter to Archbishop Cushing of Boston, published in the *American Ecclesiastical Review*, 77 (1952), pp. 307–311.

may be helped in understanding their faith and explaining it to non-Christians. The following seem to me to be important points:

1. The fact that men can be saved outside the Catholic Church is no longer disputed by anybody. The Second Vatican Council has explicitly affirmed this in the new Constitution on the Church (November 21, 1964): "But if some men do not know the Father of our Lord Jesus Christ, yet acknowledge the Creator, or seek the unknown God in shadows and images, then God himself is not far from such men, since he gives life and inspiration to all (cf. Acts 17:25–28), and the Saviour wills that all men should be saved (cf. 1 Tim. 2:4). Those who, while guiltlessly ignorant of Christ's Gospel and of his Church, sincerely seek God and are brought by the influence of grace to perform his will as known by the dictates of conscience, can achieve eternal salvation. Nor does divine Providence deny the assistance necessary to salvation to those who, without having attained, through no fault of their own, to an explicit knowledge of God, are striving, not without divine grace, to lead a good life" (*De Ecclesia* II, 16).

2. But precisely because it is possible for people to be saved outside the Church, this axiom, in its negative, exclusive formulation, continues time after time, no matter what efforts are made to explain it, to occasion innumerable misunderstandings both inside and outside the Catholic Church. While it may have helped the Church and her mission:

a. Such a concept of the Church contradicts the way in which the Church is understood in the New Testament and in Christian tradition as derived from it.

b. As has already been said, such a concept of the Church is in no way necessary in order to see the possibility of the salvation of non-Christians.

c. Such a concept of the Church makes it unnecessarily

difficult for missionaries to preach to non-Christians about joining the community of the Church, since they would have to preach at the same time that all men of good will are already in the Church.

d. Such a concept of the Church is rightly rejected by thinking non-Christians as a piece of pure theological construction and speculation; they feel that it is a somewhat impudent notion in us Christians, when they explicitly and of their own full volition do not choose to be members of the Church of Christ, to incorporate them tacitly in the Church against their will and their express choice, as though this were something that could be done over their heads.

The problem of the salvation of non-Christians is not to be solved by a theological construct.

3. The basic *theological* solution, to which we must next turn our attention, is to be found in a positive assessment of the significance of the world religions in relation to God's universal plan of salvation, and hence in a consideration, proceeding from the New Testament, of the place and task of the Church in that world which is not of the Church. This involves, in contrast to the statement that "Outside the Church there is no salvation," the working out not of the Church's claims upon the world and dominion over it, but her service of the world. In other words, the Church is to be understood not as a closed society of those in possession, but an open community of those who serve and help. We shall return to this in a moment.

4. As a preliminary *practical* solution of how to handle the axiom itself, the following suggest themselves to me:

a. In *dogmatic* teaching, the statement is to be preserved as an expression of Catholic tradition and at the same time exhibited in all its limitation and liability to misunderstanding. It should be emphasized that the crucial point is that salvation is given to us in Christ and in him alone, whether a person of good will ultimately finds himself inside or outside the visible communion of those who believe in and confess Christ.

b. In *preaching*, this statement should be as far as possible set aside and not used, because it causes more misunderstanding than understanding. The history of the ecumenical Councils teaches us that this kind of thing has often happened. The Council of Nicaea worked on the supposition that there is only one hypostasis in God. Later ecumenical Councils abandoned this formula, because it gave rise to misunderstanding, and spoke of one physis and three hypostases. As in the doctrine of the Trinity, so in Christology: The Council of Chalcedon deliberately avoided the use of certain Christological formulae which had been used at the Council of Ephesus under the influence of Cyril of Alexandria. Thus, even at that date the Church distinguished—to quote John XXIII—between the content of faith and the form in which it is clothed. The dress can change, the faith remains the same. We believe in salvation through Christ in the Church. But the formula "Outside the Church no salvation," easy to misunderstand and damaging to the Church's mission, should, for the sake of this very faith, no longer be used.

This somewhat negatively critical look at the ecclesiocentric view has prepared the ground for a positive and constructive presentation of the theocentric view.

God's Free and All-Embracing Grace

How does the destiny of non-Christian mankind appear if we look, not primarily at the Church, but at God; if we

consider non-Christian mankind not from the point of view
of the Church's system but from that of God's will and plan
for salvation; if, that is, we proceed not from *intra* to *extra*
but from *extra* to *intra*?

Non-Christians often accuse the Bible of intolerance. The
God of the Bible is said to be exclusive, the God only of
Jews and Christians. Is this true? It cannot, most certainly,
be disputed that the Old and New Testaments are far removed from any kind of superficial indifferentism. They are
totally focused on conversion to, and faith in, the one God
of Abraham, Isaac and Jacob, the God and Father of Jesus
Christ. But does this involve intolerance and exclusiveness?
Does this mean that the God of the Bible is the God of a
part of mankind only, a superior sort of tribal god? Let us
take a closer look. What judgment is passed upon pagans by
the Old Testament, by Jesus himself, and finally by apostolic
preaching?

1. *The Old Testament.* According to the Old Testament,
pagans are clearly under the wrath and judgment of God. If
they are to find grace and salvation they must be converted
to the God of Israel. Within this perspective of *metanoia*,
the Old Testament has no explicit interest in depicting pagan
religion and morality as having any positive value. On the
contrary, negative descriptions and condemnations of paganism of the most extreme kind abound in the Old Testament, especially in the preaching of the prophets, where they
are often mingled with threats. Such forceful vigor was
needed to maintain the little people of Israel in its unique
monotheism and elevated ethics amid the polytheism and
the many kinds of moral laxity of its neighbors.

But there were two streams of tradition in the Old Testament out of which, despite the weight of national partic-

ularism, there began to develop with greater and greater clarity a more open, universalist view of the pagan peoples:

a. In the first place, this same *prophetical* preaching is always essentially a self-criticism of the people of Israel as well, with the pagan peoples often appearing as those who are fulfilling the divine will. While certainly not the main, nevertheless an important subsidiary line in this preaching expresses the idea that God's "grace" and "justice" extend beyond Israel. The pagan world, too, stands in the shadow of his justice and his grace, of which the whole earth is full (Ps. 33:5; 119:64). This universalist thinking, already discernible in the prophet Amos, reaches its first peak in Isaiah. It is then continued by Jeremiah, Ezechiel and especially Deutero-Isaiah, who most magnificently of all proclaims the participation of the pagans in eschatological salvation through the Servant of God, the Light of the Gentiles. Universalism underwent a modification, in Daniel and the apocalyptic writers, through the doctrine of the ages of the world; and in later Judaism universalist thought tended to become obscured by political and apocalyptic ideas of revenge against oppressors.

b. Alongside this world-wide prophetical hope of salvation, we have the *priestly tradition*, in which the election of the people of Israel is always seen against the background of God's creation of the world and dominion over it: a world order within which God grants access to himself both to Israel and to the pagan peoples. It is significant that the Old Testament does not simply begin with the history of the people of Israel, or the choosing of Abraham. Even before Abraham there is salvation history and covenant history, a salvation history and covenant history of the *whole* of mankind. History begins not with the first Israelite but with

"man" (Adam). It is not only Israelites but man as a whole
—and this is a tremendous statement—who is "made in the
image and likeness of God" (Gen. 1:26f.). It is not only the
sinful Israelite but man as a whole who, in the teaching of
the Jahvist, receives after the Fall the promise of the Seed
who will crush the head of the serpent (Gen. 3:15). Again,
according to the priestly document, the covenant with Noah
is made with the whole of mankind: a universal, cosmic
alliance with "every living creature on earth" (Gen. 9:10;
cf. 9:11, 16f.), and an eternally valid covenant, "forever"
(9:12; cf. 9:16). The enumeration of all the peoples of the
earth which immediately follows upon the story of Noah,
the Table of the Nations in Genesis 10, unique in antiquity,
gives explicit re-emphasis to this universal character of the
covenant: the whole of mankind appears here, in terms of its
common origin, as one family. Then, within this Noachite
covenant which embraces all men, the particular covenant
is made with Abraham, as the answer to the confusion of
tongues at Babel: this is the beginning of the special choosing
of one people, but, again, this people is to serve all mankind
—an idea which already makes its appearance in connection
with the name of Abraham, by whom "all the families of the
earth shall bless themselves" (Gen. 12:3; 28:14). We thus
have a vast panorama of history within which the covenant
idea is presented in two concentric circles: the Noachite
covenant for the whole of mankind and the covenant with
Abraham for Israel alone. What the first chapters of Genesis
aim at giving, set over against the history of Israel, is not a
scientific or historical account of the beginnings of things
but, through a reaching-back behind the accounts of Israel's
origin to the source of all history in God, an all-embracing
universalist vision of the whole of salvation history is bound

up with the history of Israel. The God of Israel's covenant thus appears as the Lord of all the world, King over every people.

God's grace thus reaches out beyond the chosen people of God: Israel's attitude toward the law of Sinai is compared with the attitude of the heathen toward the statutes appointed for them (Ezek. 5:6); from the rising of the sun to its setting God's name is great among the nations, and in every place a pure offering is made to him (Mal. 1:11); even the worship of the heavenly bodies is referred to an ordinance which God has made for the heathen (Deut. 4:19). The later Wisdom literature becomes explicit in saying that the Gentiles too have a share in that wisdom of God which is revealed in creation itself, which is thus available to all peoples and constitutes a bridge between Israel's knowledge of wisdom and that of the heathen peoples (cf. especially Proverbs 8). Given this whole perspective, it is not astonishing that a whole series of "holy pagans" is to be found in the Old Testament: Abel, Enoch, Daniel, Noah, Job, Melchizedek, Lot, the Queen of Sheba. There are other pagans too who appear in a kindly light in the Old Testament: the Canaanite women Shua and Tamar (Gen. 38:2), Joseph's wife Asenath (Gen. 4:50), Pharaoh's daughter (Ex. 2:5), Moses' father-in-law Jethro (Ex. 18), Rachab (Jos. 2:1–21), Ruth, Ithra (II Sam. 17:25), the sailors in the story of Jonah (Jon. 1:16), and the mixed multitude that was with the people in their journey through the desert (Num. 11:4), etc. Taking it all together, it is clear that outside Israel there is by no means only wrath and darkness, error and sin, but that here too, in a hidden way, God's grace reigns and is at work. God and his plan of salvation are greater and more comprehensive than Israel; that plan is directed toward the whole

of mankind. How is the preaching of Jesus now to be seen
against the background of the Old Testament?

2. *The Preaching of Jesus.* Although, in the one saying on
the subject that has been transmitted to us, Jesus passed a
very negative judgment on the extremely intensive Jewish missionary work of his time (Mt. 23:15), and though—apart from
the Roman centurion, the Syro-Phoenician woman and the
possessed man at Gerasa, exceptions which prove the rule—
he limited his own activity to Israel (Mt. 15:24) and forbade
his disciples, during his own lifetime, to preach to non-Jews
(Mt. 10:5f.), yet his judgment on the Gentiles was fundamentally different from the completely negative judgment
passed upon them by his contemporaries, who saw them as
quite unquestionably godless and rejected by God. Not only
does he reject all nationalistic feelings of hatred against
Romans and Samaritans and, in particular, exclude from the
eschatological hope any idea of revenge against the Gentiles;
he even promises to the Gentiles a share in salvation: not
only will the Gentiles rise again—an inconceivable thing to
many Jews—but, still more inconceivable, they will hear their
acquittal pronounced at the Judgment by the Son of Man
(Mt. 25:31–34). Both Jews and Gentiles will be judged, not
according to their origin, but solely according to their having
practiced or not practiced love toward their neighbor (Mt.
25:35–46). The pagan inhabitants of Ninive come out of this
better than the Israelites (Mt. 12:41f.; cf. on Tyre and Sidon,
and even Sodom, Mt. 11:21–24). Thus it is possible for the
Gentiles to take the place of the children of Abraham—a
monstrous threat in the ears of Jesus' contemporaries. This
is the sense of the Messianic title: Jesus manifests himself
toward *all* peoples as Son of Man (cf. Dan. 7), Prince of
Peace (cf. Zach. 9:9) and Servant of God (cf. Deutero-
Isaiah).

3. *The Apostolic Preaching.* What was, for Jesus, something that would become a full reality for all peoples only
through God's eschatological deed in the joyful feast of fulfillment, is already begun (the Last Age having already
dawned) by the mission of the Church with its demand for
a decision of faith. The infant Church finally struggled
through to consciousness of this mission chiefly under the
influence of Paul. Paul himself made his most explicit statements about the pagan world in the first two chapters of the
Epistle to the Romans, interpretation of which is a matter
of vigorous dispute. We cannot enter here into the complex
problem of "natural theology." That God exists, that he is
as a matter of fact acknowledged by men, are things which
Paul does not prove but, like the whole of the Old and New
Testaments, takes for granted as obvious. Romans 1 and 2
are certainly not favorable statements about the pagan world
at the level of abstract natural theology. Paul is not calling
on man to remain in paganism but to believe in the message
of Christ's salvation. Thus what we find in Romans 1 and
2 is not some abstract "pure nature" which, precisely as
"pure," does not exist, but man as he exists in the concrete,
the pagan world as it exists in the concrete. Hence Paul's
clear affirmation of revelation in creation (Rom. 1:18–21) is
concerned with the righteousness or wrath of God, salvation
or damnation, thanksgiving or godlessness, faith or disbelief.
Although summoned to it by God's revelation in creation,
the pagans—according to the general condemnation in Romans 1—have not glorified and given thanks to God, but
degraded the truth. Knowledge of God by the pagans without any special revelation is unambiguously affirmed in
Romans 1. Again, the line of argument in Romans 2 is directed toward the basic affirmation that *all* men, Jews and
pagans alike, are under the dominion of sin (3:9–20) and

need justification in Christ Jesus (3:21–31). But this does not
amount to a judgment on the salvation or damnation of an
individual pagan. For the question being asked here is not
about the fate of individual pagans before Christ but about
the responsibility and guilt of both groups of pre-Christian
mankind, Jews and Gentiles. The more positive undertones
in Romans 2 are unmistakable. Paul's basic affirmation is
"Glory and honor and peace for every one who does good,
the Jew first and also the Greek. For God shows no partiality"
(2:10f.). Hence what is *ultimately* important is not who has
and who has not received a special revelation—a scandalous
state to a Jew. Whether with the Law or without the Law,
"it is not the hearers of the law who are righteous before
God, but the doers of the law who will be justified" (2:13).
But how can men to whom the special revelation, the "law,"
has not been preached, be "doers of the law"? Paul answers,
because "what the law requires is written on their hearts,
while their conscience also bears witness" (2:15). And this
means that whenever (*ótan*, not an unreal condition!) "Gentiles who have not the law do by nature what the law requires,
they are a law to themselves, even though they do not have
the law" (2:14). But for Paul, conscience and faith are very
closely connected (the identical question about eating meat
offered to idols is discussed in Romans 14 in terms of "faith"
and in 1 Corinthians 8:10 in terms of "conscience").

Even more positive is what is said of the pagans in Paul's
missionary speeches as given by Luke in the Acts of the
Apostles, at Lystra (14:8–18) and Athens (17:16–34). The
object of these speeches is never, of course, that their hearers
should remain in paganism, but that they should be converted to faith in the true God (14:51; 17:30f.). But at the
same time there is an evident effort to excuse the pagans

as far as possible: God has "in past generations allowed all the nations to walk in their own ways" (14:16), he has "overlooked the times of ignorance" (17:30). There is no mention, as in Romans 1:20, of the pagans as "without excuse." At Lystra, Paul says explicitly that God "did not leave himself without witness" to the pagans, since he poured out to them the gifts of creation and filled their hearts with thankful joy (14, 17). Further, at Athens Paul recognizes a religious desire, awe of the gods (17:22), and in it—in the worship of the unknown god—an obscure, unconscious awareness of God (17, 23). But if this awareness became misdirected (in the temple cult, 17:24, in the failure to recognize that God has no need of anything, 17:25, in the cult of images, 17:29), so that pagans are in "ignorance" and are "to repent" (17:30), yet even without having been preached to, they are nevertheless not forsaken by God. For God is near to every human being—a thought already expressed in Romans 1–2, and here strengthened by the stress on the unity of the human race (17:26): "He is not far from each one of us, for 'In him we live and move and have our being'; and even some of your poets have said, 'For we are indeed his offspring' " (17:27). It can hardly be supposed from this text that those pagans who, in reverence for the gods, have an obscure awareness of God and who "seek God, in the hope that they might feel after him and find him" (17:27), will simply remain unfulfilled in their seeking unless they encounter the word preached by the apostles. In practicing their religion they are, in actual fact, being concerned with the true and merciful God. The Epistle to the Hebrews testifies, without suggesting any special revelation, to the faith of Abel (11:4), Enoch (11:5) and the harlot Rhab (11:31).

Finally, according to the Johannine prologue the divine

Logos, within the creation which has come to be through him, is already life and light for men in the darkness (Jn. 1:4f.). The creator is simultaneously the revealer. The Logos has a universal function of revelation: "The true light that enlightens *every* man was coming into the world" (1:9). But "the world knew him not" (1:10). Plainly, a distinction has to be made here between the enlightenment given everywhere and at all times through the Word abiding with God, and the calling of the community to God through the man Jesus.

We shall have to forego at this point any further examination of the findings of exegesis—it is very complex material and necessarily, from the very nature of the problem, dialectically negative-positive in character. At any rate, we have arrived at a stage where the following points are clear:

1. In the light of the universalist testimonies that pervade the Old and New Testaments it is quite impossible to maintain that the Bible takes a purely negative attitude of exclusive intolerance toward other religions.

2. It is perfectly clear that the God of the Bible is not only the God of Jews and Christians but the God of all men.

3. The *negative* statements concerning the error, darkness, lies and sin of the pagan world refer to paganism insofar as it sets itself against the saving will of God. These negative statements are to be understood not as a definitive sentence of damnation but as a call to conversion addressed to the pagans of the present day. The fate of earlier pagans, or those not confronted with the revelation of Christ, is of only indirect interest to the Bible.

4. The *positive* statements about the pagan world show that there exists a primitive, original communication of God to the whole of mankind. This is something asserted explicitly by individual witnesses, and assumed throughout the Bible:

the Gentiles can know the God of grace. This knowledge of God is not simply a self-sufficient human activity of "natural theology," but a response to the basic revelation of the God of grace in creation, of which man is himself, in the first instance, a part. Thus even before their encounter with the Gospel of Christ, there is already a history of God's presence to the pagan peoples, a history in which decisions are taken. There is no explicit answer in the Bible to the question of who, among those pagans untouched by the Gospel, are saved. But it is certain that even in the darkness of paganism God is near to every human being, is indeed necessary for his very life.

The Second Vatican Council has Scripture as its support when it affirms:

> One is the community of all peoples, one their origin, for God made the whole human race to live over the face of the earth. One also is their final goal, God. His providence, His manifestations of goodness, His saving design extend to all men, until that time when the elect will be united in the Holy City, the city ablaze with the glory of God, where the nations will walk in His light.*

Such, then, is the perspective of this problem when the starting-point is not the Church but God's will and plan for salvation, as it is made known to us, and so far as it is made known to us, in Scripture. The question of what lies outside the Church is one which can be asked but, as we have seen, is difficult to answer. As to what lies outside God and his plan of salvation, this is not a real question at all. If we look

---

* Second Vatican Council's *Declaration on the Relation of the Church to Non-Christian Religions*, 1.

at God's plan of salvation, then there is no *extra*, only an *intra*; no outside, only an inside, for "God desires *all* men to be saved and to come to the knowledge of the truth. For there is *one* God, and there is *one* mediator between God and men, the man Christ Jesus, who gave himself as a ransom for *all*" (1 Tim. 2:4–6).

Within this great and gracious, all-embracing *intra*, this inside, it is now possible to give positive account of the relationship of the world religions to the Church and of the Church to the world religions.

Christian Universalism

We are taking the concept of "religion" as widely as possible. We include in it not only the theistic religions, which acknowledge a God or several gods, but also the non-theistic religions, which ascribe divine attributes to a supreme principle or an all-pervading power or energy. Indirectly and analogously we even include what Paul Tillich called "quasi-religions," in which it is perfectly possible for men of good will to be gripped by something which is for them an ultimate concern (or "idea"), to which all other concerns are subordinate and which gives to the lives of such people their ultimate meaning: e.g., national concern in nationalism; social concern in Communism; liberal-humane concern in liberal humanism with its faith in science. These "quasi-religions" can also be called "substitute religions," thus drawing attention to their underlying deficiency. But the term is not to be taken as involving any automatic disqualification of the honest intentions and good faith of those who serve such an "idea," often with utter commitment.

It is impossible to overlook the fact that, on the one hand, these quasi-religions, turning to their own account the secularization and religious indifference which go with technology and industrialization, constitute a greater threat to Christianity than the real religions, theistic or non-theistic, and that, on the other hand, the quasi-religions are also at present a greater threat to the non-Christian religions than are the Christian missions. From this point of view too, a dialogue between the Church and the real religions would seem to be called for. But this threat must not cause us to overlook the fact that even the quasi-religions, because of their positive elements and concerns, can have a religious character for men of good will. Hence, while they will not be dealt with directly in our consideration of world religions (the problem they present being in other respects very different from that of the real religions), yet they must be at least indirectly included. What, fundamentally, then, have we, as Christians, to say of the world religions?

1. We confess right from the start that we are trying to answer this question from the *Christian* standpoint. And no one has a right to describe this, in advance, as intolerant and exclusive. It may indeed be described as a "dogmatic" standpoint. On this, it should simply be said that in this sense the non-Christian religions, too, proceed from a "dogmatic" or "absolute" standpoint. If we set aside early primitive religions and religious experiences, and the religions of myth, achieving a general view of reality, which succeeded them, and confine ourselves to religions which have in some way broken out of myth, we can then distinguish, phenomenologically, three types in the development of religions. They *all* have a "dogmatic" starting-point.*

It is a *dogmatic* type of religion, first appearing in Greece

---

* Cf. J. Ratzinger, "Der christliche Glaube und die Weltreligionen," in *Gott in Welt. Festschrift Karl Rahner* (Freiburg-Basel-Vienna, 1964), vol. 2, pp. 287–305.

but particularly successful in modern times in the form of
the *Enlightenment,* which discards myth as a pre-scientific
form of knowledge while erecting *rational,* "*scientific*" *knowledge* into an absolute and subordinating everything in the
religious field to it.

But the religions at the opposite pole to this are also dogmatic: those taking the form of "mysticism," to which the
myths are mere symbols—perhaps to be seen through as
illusory, perhaps to be preserved—while it is the *inner, formless, mystical experience of the divine* which is made into
an absolute. When, for instance, Radhakrishnan, whose religious mysticism includes a number of characteristics belonging rather to the Enlightenment, affirms that there is in the
endless multiplicity of religions, in their forms and languages,
an underlying identity which makes possible a profound spiritual communion between the various religions, this is entirely unobjectionable. But when he simplifies this identity
to the point of asserting that all articulate religious statements,
all revelations and confessions of faith, all authorities and
rites are relative, and the *only* thing that has any ultimate
validity is that inner spiritual experience of the absolute which
appears in different forms in all religions and can never be
adequately expressed, then he is taking up a dogmatic standpoint. It is only possible to make all religions *equal* if the
underlying, formless, mystical experience is being set up as an
absolute. We Christians are reproached with preaching to
non-Christians the absoluteness of the revelation made in
Jesus Christ. But do we have to feel that it is any more
tolerant, are we not bound to feel it almost as a declaration
of war on all forms of faith which are historical in their way
of thinking, when someone seeks to impose upon us the
absolute of an ultimate, exclusively valid mystical experience,
with no room for anything superior to it?

Ultimately, it has to be a decision of faith—and we Christians hold that we have sufficient grounds for the one we make—which of the two is to be regarded as decisive: the mystic's *experience of identity*, striving to be immersed in the monist All-and-One, described both as "nothing" and as "all," or the *otherness* of the God who calls us, as experienced by the prophet not in absorption by him but in obedience to his call. And hence whether we understand God, as in the religions of mysticism, as the purely *passive*, in relation to whom man is active (through absorption, immersion, ascent, union), or whether we understand God, whom the very purest among us cannot, of himself, discover, as the truly *active*, who acts upon man and so brings him to activity. And hence again whether one accords preference to the "great religious personalities" and ascetics who have achieved perfect interiority, or to the simple ministers of the Word, whose desire is to be obedient in faith to the revealing Word. Whether, then, one ultimately reduces the person to the *impersonal* or, as we do, the impersonal to the *person*; whether one ultimately takes the non-historical way of dissolving all history in the identity of eternal recurrence, or, as we do, seeks to understand history truly *historically* as progress toward a goal.

As against the religions of enlightenment and the religions of mysticism, then, Christianity, considered simply in terms of a phenomenology of religion, appears as a way whose starting-point is neither more nor less "dogmatic" than that of other religions. If even the sceptic—which Radhakrishnan is not—claims to be able to assert his scepticism and to contradict those who question its validity, then the Christian may also claim to be able to defend the reality of God's call in Christ and to contradict those who dispute it. The Christian way, as Ratzinger rightly describes it, is the mature version of something that arose in Israel and was taken up

again in the post-Christian era by Mohammedanism: "revolutionary monotheism," which regards as the absolute
neither rational scientific knowledge nor ineffable religious
experience, but the divine summons made in the prophet;
but which does not—like other, evolutionary forms of monotheism—tend toward an equation of God with the gods,
belief in one god with belief in many gods, but, by hearing
God's summons, has achieved a revolutionary smashing of
myth and overthrowing of the gods of myth.

I am not concerned here to make an apologetical defense
of our faith, for which there seem to be many interior grounds,
but simply to demonstrate that our particular starting-point
is not to be regarded in advance as illegitimate. The non-
Christian peoples of Asia, who have adopted Western science,
technology, political democracy and thus—whether they like
it or not—a whole series of secularized Christian ideas, will
be able to see for themselves whether, through what they
have thus taken over, a certain correction of their religious
convictions in a Christian direction is imposing itself: a correction, for instance, of cosmic pessimism and of anti-historical
cosmic cyclism; the setting of a higher value on the visible
world, on the individual and concrete, on the individual person, on the equality of all men; the positive evaluation of a
non-cyclic, progressive historical process, of the necessity of
reforming the world, of practical social love of neighbor, of
history as having a goal, etc.

2. Now, given the legitimacy of the Christian starting-
point, what has the Christian faith to say of the world religions? The Old and New Testaments do indeed treat of
the peoples, but not of the religions as such. Nevertheless, the
biblical material on the evaluation of paganism, which we have
tried to elucidate a little, gives us a good foundation on which
to summarize our conception in thesis form.

a. *Despite whatever truth they have concerning the true God, the world religions are in error.* We do not need to go over what the Old and New Testaments say of the error, lies, sin and darkness of the pagan world. Nor do we need to bring together, from the material supplied by comparative religion, the appalling evidence which supports this negative judgment. All this is an expression of estrangement from God and from him whom the gracious God has sent, and who is not only light but *the* Light, not only truth but *the* Truth. Hence the Gospel of Jesus Christ demands not the fulfillment of the world religions but a metanoia, a conversion and return from false gods to the true God in Jesus Christ.

b. *The world religions do, though in error, proclaim the truth of the true God.* Though they are far from God, God is not far from them. Though they flee from the true God, they are yet graciously held by him who is their God too. By him they are made able, in the midst of all their errors, to speak truly of him. The grace of the true God can witness to itself even through false gods, and can trace the image of the true God even through its misplaced and dissociated features. The grace of the true God is able to make mere service of idols count as concealed worship of God, and mere erroneous, confused and superstitious belief or unbelief count as hidden faith. Hence in its summons to conversion the Gospel of Jesus Christ does not require the renunciation of whatever in the world religions "is true, whatever is honorable, whatever is just, whatever is pure, whatever is lovely, whatever is gracious" (Phil. 4:8).

c. *As against the "extraordinary" way of salvation which is the Church, the world religions can be called the "ordinary" way of salvation for non-Christian humanity.* God is the Lord not only of the special salvation history of the Church, but also of that other salvation history: the universal salvation history of all mankind. This universal salvation history is bound up with special salvation history in a common origin, meaning and goal, and is subject to the same grace of God. Every historical situation, outside the Church as well as inside it, is thus included in advance within his grace. Since, as a matter of Christian faith, the true God seriously and effectively wills that *all* men should be saved and none lost unless by his own fault, every man is intended to find his salvation within his *own* historical condition. "Within his own historical condition," means here, within his particular individual and social environment, from which he cannot simply escape; it means, finally, within the religion socially imposed on him from which, equally, he cannot normally simply escape. Man's religion, as the religion of a social being who is essentially social, is never merely an individualist, subjectivist activity in a purely private interior zone, but always an activity in a particular social embodiment, i.e., in the form of a particular religion, a concrete religious community.

But since God seriously and effectively wills the universal salvation history of the whole of mankind, although he does not, indeed, legitimize every element (some being erroneous and depraved) in these religions (even the Old Covenant was not perfect!), yet he does sanction the *religions as such* —as social structures. These, although in different senses and degrees, are in their own way "legitimate religions."* A man is to be saved within the religion that is made available to him in his historical situation, which, for the man in question, is not merely an external framework but, if it is *genuine*, forms a part of himself. Hence it is his right and his duty to seek God within that religion in which the hidden God has already found him. All this until such time as he is con-

* See K. Rahner, "Das Christentum und die nichtchristlichen Religionen," *Schriften zur Theologie* 5 (Einsiedeln-Zürich-Cologne, 1962), pp. 147–154.

fronted in an existential way with the revelation of Jesus Christ. The religions with their forms of belief and cult, their categories and values, their symbols and ordinances, their religious and ethical experience, thus have a "relative validity"* and a "relative providential right to existence."† Through the grace of the one God they can be—though they need not necessarily be—the *way of salvation* within universal salvation history. When, and where, and how they actually are this does not come within the scope of our judgment. But through the grace of the one God they can be the way of salvation. Considering the incomparably greater number of people in the world religions, compared with which Christendom is a small minority, we can speak of these religions as the general, the "ordinary," way of salvation, beside which the way of salvation in the Church appears as something altogether special and extraordinary: the way of the Church can be seen as the high and excellent and "extraordinary" way of salvation! It is thus that we today, on the basis of our clearer insight into mankind's historical situation and into the universalist perspective of the Christian message, can adapt our former theological terminology (though the question is not primarily one of terminology): the way of salvation for mankind outside the Church can be described as the "ordinary" way, that within the Church as the "extraordinary" way of salvation.‡

d. *The world religions teach truth about the Gospel of Christ, which, in their error, they do not know as that which it really is: the Truth.*

1. Despite their errors the religions teach the truth of

* Cf. J. Neuner, "Missionstheologische Probleme in Indien," in *Gott in Welt. Festschift Karl Rahner* (Freiburg-Basel-Vienna, 1964), 2, 401f.

† H. R. Schlette, *Die Religionen als Thema der Theologie* (Freiburg-Basel-Vienna, 1963), p. 39.

‡ *Ibid.*, p. 85.

Christ when, in a multitude of insights, they recognize *man's need of salvation*; when they discern the loneliness, the helpless and forlorn state of man in this world, his abysmal fear and distress, his evil behavior and false pride; when they see the cruelty, perdition and nothingness of this world, and the meaning and meaninglessness of death; when, because of this, they look for something new, and long for a transformation, a rebirth and a redemption of man and his world.

2. Despite their errors, the religions teach the truth of Christ when they recognize *God's graciousness*: when, that is, they know that the Godhead, for all its nearness, is far off and hidden, that it is the divine itself which must grant us its nearness, presence and accessibility; when they know, then, that man cannot draw near to it by himself, relying on his own innocence, but that he needs to be purified and reconciled, that he can only arrive at life through death, that sacrifice is needed for the purging of guilt; more, that man cannot redeem himself but is dependent on the loving mercy of God.

3. Despite all their error, the religions are teaching the truth of Christ when they listen to the *voice of their prophets*: when they thus, through their prophets, receive courage and strength for a new break-through into greater truth and deeper knowledge, into a revival and renewal of religion as it has been handed down.

Thus, the world religions make a constant claim on the Church's thoughtful attention: confronted by the manifold *falsity* in the world religions, the Church can reach a new and thankful awareness of the grace of her special election; but confronted by the manifold truth in the world religions, she must become humbly aware of her own numerous betrayals and constant falling-short of the message of her Lord.

e. *It is the Gospel of Jesus Christ that is able to liberate* the truth of the world religions from their entanglement in error and sin. Though the religions do in many ways proclaim the truth of Christ, yet they do not know him whose truth they proclaim; in all their proclamation of truth they fail to recognize him who, as the Father's Word, is *the* Truth. It is this which, despite the light which they shed at very many different points, constitutes their basic darkness, in which they themselves cannot see, and which can only be illuminated by him who is *the* Light.

1. The religions are structures which, because of God's gracious revelation of himself in creation, are light, and at the same time, because of man's failure to recognize the true God in Christ, are darkness. Thus they are *not* "natural theology," "natural piety," "natural morality," but are sharply ambiguous: on the one hand embraced, upheld and penetrated by God's grace, and yet, on the other hand, in the bonds and oppression of man's betrayal and wickedness. It is only necessary to look at the history of religion in the concrete to see all the appalling error and moral weakness, to see how little these religions know of the true nature of God and the true nature of man, how constantly they fall either into an abrupt dualistic separation or an overweening monistic union with him. How often, for instance, in Hinduism is the reality of the free and living God either exaggerated in its transcendence into the impersonal absolute or esoteric philosophers or reduced, in its encounter with man, to the anthropomorphic, materialized object of a ritualistic and magical popular piety! Similar things could be said of the Hindu understanding of sin and redemption, of law and of providence.* However inappropriate that arrogant lack of understanding may be which rejects the world religions as

* Cf. Neuner, *op. cit.*, pp. 405–9; also *Hinduismus und Christentum. Eine Einführung*, ed. J. Neuner (Vienna-Freiburg-Basel, 1962).

simply false, it is no less inappropriate to idealize them in
utopian fashion as uniformly perfect objectivizations of man's
religious experience. Within every true message uttered by
the world religions there always lingers the illusion of myth;
in all their yearning for God there remains a denial and flight
from God; in all their hope for God's grace, a concealed self-
redemption; in all their genuine conversion, an inadvertent
turning-away. The world religions all stand in need of demythologizing and the casting out of devils, of interiorizing
and humanizing. As non-Christian religions, though they are
certainly not simply un-Christian, yet they are pre-Christian,
directed toward Christ. And again, it is better not to call these
pre-Christian religions "anonymously Christian," because it
is precisely they *themselves* who do not know their own
Christian character, though Christ does not deny his presence
to them. The men of the world religions are not Christians
by profession, but by designation, by vocation, and in some
sense already by their affirmative response.

2. Only the preaching of the Gospel of Jesus Christ is
able in this situation to bring light and to dissipate darkness,
to liberate the truth which is here to a large extent oppressed
and held in bondage. The Gospel of Jesus Christ lights up
the point of man's deepest need, and shows where his real
salvation is to be found, what God really means for men and
what man really has to be in the sight of God, what the real
communion is between God and man. This is what, at bottom, the world religions cannot know. They do not believe
in and confess him who alone can give them this knowledge
in faith. The world religions are only religions; they are not
churches, for this means a community of those who believe
in Christ and confess him. But the individual people in the
world religions are called upon existentially by the Church

of Christ to make the decision of faith in Christ only at that point in time when they are reached not only by some report or information about the Gospel of Jesus Christ, but by the preaching of that Gospel itself. Much non-belief is not an unbelieving rejection of the message of salvation but merely an inadequate encounter with a message not possessing, for this particular man, the inviting and demanding force of revelation.

What we have said up to this point is in accord with Vatican II when it states:

Men expect from the various religions answers to the unsolved riddles of the human condition, which today, even as in former times, deeply stir the hearts of men: What is man? What is the meaning, the aim of our life? What is moral good, what sin? Whence suffering and what purpose does it serve? Which is the road to true happiness? What are death, judgment and retribution after death? What, finally, is that ultimate inexpressible mystery which encompasses our existence: whence do we come, and where are we going?

From ancient times down to the present, there is found among various peoples a certain perception of that hidden power which hovers over the course of things and over the events of human history; at times some indeed have come to the recognition of a Supreme Being, or even of a Father. This perception and recognition penetrates their lives with a profound religious sense.

Religions, however, that are bound up with an advanced culture have struggled to answer the same ques-

tions by means of more refined concepts and a more
developed language. Thus in Hinduism, men contem-
plate the divine mystery and express it through an inexhaustible abundance of myths and through searching
philosophical inquiry. They seek freedom from the an-
guish of our human condition either through ascetical
practices or profound meditation or a flight to God with
love and trust. Again, Buddhism, in its various forms,
realizes the radical insufficiency of this changeable world;
it teaches a way by which men, in a devout and confident
spirit, may be able either to acquire the state of perfect
liberation, or attain, by their own efforts or through
higher help, supreme illumination. Likewise, other religions found everywhere try to counter the restlessness of
the human heart, each in its own manner, by proposing
"ways," comprising teachings, rules of life, and sacred
rites.

The Catholic Church rejects nothing that is true and
holy in these religions. She regards with sincere reverence
those ways of conduct and of life, those precepts and
teachings which, though differing in many aspects from
the ones she holds and sets forth, nonetheless often re-
flect a ray of that Truth which enlightens all men.
Indeed, she proclaims, and ever must proclaim Christ,
"the way, the truth, and the life" (John 14:6), in whom
men may find the fullness of religious life, in whom God
has reconciled all things to Himself.

The Church, therefore, exhorts her sons, that through
dialogue and collaboration with the followers of other
religions, carried out with prudence and love and in wit-

ness to the Christian faith and life, they recognize, preserve and promote the good things, spiritual and moral, as well as the socio-cultural values found among these men.*

f. *Christian faith represents radical universalism, but one grounded and made concrete in, and centered upon, Jesus Christ.* This radical universalism means, as has already been said:

1. Every human being is under God's grace and can be saved: whether he be of this or that nation or race, of this or that caste or class, free or slave, man or woman, or even inside or outside the Church of Christ. Every human being can be saved, and we may hope that everyone is.

2. Every world religion is under God's grace and can be a way of salvation: whether it is primitive or highly evolved, mythological or enlightened, mystical or rational, theistic or non-theistic, a real or only a quasi-religion. Every religion can be a way of salvation and we may hope that every one is.

But we Christians in the Church of Christ believe this not on the basis of an indefinable, unaccountable mystical experience, which can in fact be a form of myth. We believe it on the basis of the message and history of Jesus Christ which has been testified to us. It is in Jesus Christ, in whom God himself has spoken and acted for all men in a unique way, that our radical universalism is grounded, centered and made concrete. Hence *Christian* universalism is equally far removed from a narrow, limited, exclusive particularism and from an enfeebling, disintegrating, agnostic, relativistic indifferentism. Hence we have nothing to say for the totalitarian *domination*

* Second Vatican Council's *Declaration on the Relation of the Church to Non-Christian Religions*, 1–2.

of one religion, which suppresses *freedom*. But neither have we anything to say for a syncretist *mingling* of all religions, which suppresses *truth*. What we believe in is *service* of the religions of the world by the Church of Jesus Christ, in love, which unites truth and freedom.

From this aspect one must also see the relationship to the religion of Israel, which will always remain a very special one since the Church of Jesus Christ stems from it. What sins Christians have committed against Jews over the centuries, have been in effect sins against the Gospel of Jesus Christ. They can only be judged, and judged severely, and we must therefore pray for forgiveness. The anti-Semitism of the National Socialists and their unparalleled crimes would have been impossible without the latent and too often vicious anti-Semitism of the Catholic and other Christian churches. Today, we must, with all our energy, seek a new, positive relationship precisely with the Jews, both in theology and practice. Here too, the Vatican Council has, in an epoch-making fashion, reversed the current of history:

> As the sacred synod searches into the mystery of the Church, it remembers the bond that spiritually ties the people of the New Covenant to Abraham's stock.
>
> Thus the Church of Christ acknowledges that, according to God's saving design, the beginnings of her faith and her election are found already among the Patriarchs, Moses and the prophets. She professes that all who believe in Christ—Abraham's sons according to faith—are included in the same Patriarch's call, and likewise that the salvation of the Church is mysteriously foreshadowed by the chosen people's exodus from the land of bondage.

The Church, therefore, cannot forget that she received the revelation of the Old Testament through the people with whom God in His inexpressible mercy concluded the Ancient Covenant. Nor can she forget that she draws sustenance from the root of that well-cultivated olive tree onto which have been grafted the wild shoots, the Gentiles. Indeed, the Church believes that by His cross Christ Our Peace reconciled Jews and Gentiles, making both one in Himself.

The Church keeps ever in mind the words of the Apostle about his kinsmen: "Theirs is the sonship and the glory and the covenants and the law and the worship and the promises; theirs are the fathers and from them is the Christ according to the flesh" (Rom. 9:4–5), the Son of the Virgin Mary. She also recalls that the Apostles, the Church's main-stay and pillars, as well as most of the early disciples who proclaimed Christ's Gospel to the world, sprang from the Jewish people.

As Holy Scripture testifies, Jerusalem did not recognize the time of her visitation, nor did the Jews, in large number, accept the Gospel; indeed not a few opposed its spreading. Nevertheless, God holds the Jews most dear for the sake of their Fathers; He does not repent of the gifts He makes or of the calls He issues—such is the witness of the Apostle. In company with the Prophets and the same Apostle, the Church awaits that day, known to God alone, on which all peoples will address the Lord in a single voice and "serve him shoulder to shoulder" (Soph. 3:9).

Since the spiritual patrimony common to Christians

and Jews is thus so great, this sacred synod wants to foster and recommend that mutual understanding and respect which is the fruit, above all, of biblical and theological studies as well as of fraternal dialogues.

True, the Jewish authorities and those who followed their lead pressed for the death of Christ; still, what happened in His passion cannot be charged against all the Jews, without distinction, then alive, nor against the Jews of today. Although the Church is the people of God, the Jews should not be presented as rejected or accursed by God, as if this followed from the Holy Scriptures. All should see to it, then, that in catechetical work or in the preaching of the word of God they do not teach anything that does not conform to the truth of the Gospel and the spirit of Christ.

Furthermore, in her rejection of every persecution against any man, the Church, mindful of the patrimony she shares with the Jews and moved not by political reasons but by the Gospel's spiritual love, decries hatred, persecutions, displays of anti-Semitism, directed against Jews at any time and by anyone.

Besides, as the Church has always held and holds now, Christ underwent His passion and death freely, because of the sins of men and out of infinite love, in order that all may reach salvation. It is, therefore, the burden of the Church's preaching to proclaim the cross of Christ as the sign of God's all-embracing love and as the fountain from which every grace flows.*

* Second Vatican Council's *Declaration on the Relation of the Church to Non-Christian Religions,* 4.

What is meant by this service by the Church of the world religions? This is the last question which we have to consider.

The Church Free for the World Religions

The Church's missionary work in the world, which should be a mission not only to Asia and Africa but in Europe too, on the frontiers not only of the world-wide church but of every parish, is today in no small danger from fear and defeatism, the fear that we are not, fundamentally, making any progress. Figures are quoted such as those quoted at the beginning of this chapter. The realization is spreading in the Catholic Church that it is not going to be possible, at least in the foreseeable future, to "convert" all the pagans, old and new, to evangelize the world religions, to Christianize the world; that on the contrary there are going to be, for the foreseeable future—and perhaps to the end of time—not only individual pagans but a pagan world, world religions, and religious pluralism.

Fear and defeatism have got to be fought against. First, the simple question has to be asked: Was what we seem to expect ever promised to us at all? Is that what we read in the Scriptures—the victory, within this world, of a triumphant church? Is it not precisely the reverse—that the Church will always be a sign of contradiction, because the contradiction is against her Lord: that the Church will be a "little flock" as against the world and its powers: that pressure against her will not diminish but increase to its greatest before the end? Is it not an illusion stemming from the Constantinian and medieval periods, rather than the promise of the Gospel, which gives us the conviction that the world religions are due to disappear through the Church's preaching, and which causes us to chase hectically after quantity and superiority of numbers? No missionary command ever laid *that* on us. Against it, there is not only a realistic analysis of the world situation. There are also all the *theological* considerations we have been making here. We can look without fear, but with sober Christian tranquility, at the situation in our missions, if we base a theology of the missions on the ideas which have been developed here: that the reason for conducting our missions is not that all those not confronted with them will be lost. That our missionary task does not therefore simply consist—as missionaries of earlier centuries, seeing it from a different historical situation, formulated it—in "saving souls" or even simply "founding churches" (*plantatio ecclesiae*). The Church's service to the world and the world religions does not have to be described as though God were not greater than the Church, as though it were not God but the Church which bestows salvation, as though God's victory need always be the victory of the Church, as though, when the Church does not conquer, God's grace cannot conquer either.

If we triumphalistically exalt the task of the Church and equate it as far as possible with the work of God himself, then we are indeed liable to fall into hopelessness and despair at the sight of the present concrete situation of the Church and her missions. This really is to ask too much of the Church. But if the Church's task is seen, modestly and realistically, as what it is: not the conquest of the world, but service to the world, then the Church is not being over-strained but, in the best sense of the word, challenged. Then there is every ground of hope for the Church and her mission.

Service of the Church to the world, service of the Church to the world religions: precisely because it is the desire of the Church to exist for God, she has to exist for the people in the world and in its religions. She was not *called out* from the religions of the world as the new Israel in order to exist for herself, but in order to be *sent back* again to the world religions. To this extent, "mission" (*missio*) belongs to the essence of her who has been called out (*ek-klesia*).

a. One way in which the Church exists for the sake of the world religions is that she *knows* what the real situation of the world religions is. This is something that the world religions do not know: whence they come, where they now stand, where they are going, what the ultimate situation is between God and man, wherein lies their own true salvation and damnation. The Church can, in her faith, know that her God is also the God of those who belong to the world religions, and that they too come from him and are returning to him; she can know that the one true God has, in pure grace, made his covenant with mankind in the world religions too, thence that Jesus Christ died and rose again for these men also, so that God's all-powerful mercy shines out over the greatness and wretchedness of the world religions too. It is only because the Church, in her faith in Jesus Christ, is able to know about the world religions, know their origin, their course, their goal, their potentialities and limitations, their nature and un-nature, that she is really able to exist for their sake. Hence it is not only a gift to the Church but also a task for her, to see the world religions and understand them for what they really are: to do this in understanding, in openness, in critical freedom and all-embracing good-will.

b. Another way in which the Church exists for the sake of the world religions is that she is *linked* with them: precisely because the Church knows and understands the world religions for what they are, it is absolutely impossible for her to hold pharisaically aloof from them. It is clear to her, from the knowledge that she has by faith, that she cannot simply conform herself to the likeness of the world religions; this would be to fail her own special service, for which she has been chosen. But in the knowledge which she has by faith of the grace of the one true God, who so loved the world that he gave his only son for it, she is, from the very beginning, profoundly linked with the world religions. The Church and the world religions together make up the whole of mankind, which, being sinful as a whole, has as a whole found God's mercy. How could she ever be unmindful of this common guilt and common grace? The Church can never seal herself off from the world religions and lead a life of her own in splendid isolation. Rather, she has to address herself to the world religions, declare herself to them, share in their needs and hopes, their advances and retreats. It is not a non-participating, unconnected church but only a church that is lovingly linked with them that can then, when the Gospel of Jesus Christ requires it, withstand and dispute with the world religions too, put a distance between herself and them precisely in order to remain with them still. Thus it is not only a gift but also a task for the Church to be in the midst of the world religions, alongside them and with them; thinking and speaking and acting in solidarity with them.

c. Another way in which the Church exists for the sake of the world religions is that she has *obligations* to them: if the Church is really linked with the world religions, then this connection is not going to be confined to thoughts and words in common; it will not be a mere passive, more or less peaceful co-existence. Co-existence will rather become pro-existence; being with each other will turn to being for each other. The Church's understanding of the world religions would be sterile, her link with them would be mere idleness, if these things did not lead to active co-responsibility. In following her Master, the Church is called to *active* service of the brotherhood, who are *all* creatures of the one Father. A church which was only living and acting for herself would not be the church of Christ. In everything that she does, however interior to herself it may seem, the Church of Christ exists toward the outside, toward humanity. The world religions, whether they know it or not, need the brotherly help of the Church. It is not only a gift but also a task for the Church to share responsibility with the world religions, past and future, not only in words, but in deeds.

To understand, to be linked, to have obligations toward the world religions: this is a concrete service for which the Church has been empowered and commissioned by her Master, in the Spirit. But if this understanding, this link, this obligation are not to be vague and random but solidly grounded and rooted, it is necessary to see them all under the aspect of the Church's primary, original commission, which consists in confessing and proclaiming Christ; in being his witnesses, and thus declaring the Gospel, the good news of the eschatological reign of God already initiated in Jesus Christ, and of the decision of faith now required for us: the message of God's grace and mercy and the justification, sanctification and vocation of sinful humanity, the message of life according to the Spirit in the new freedom from law, sin and death, in faith and love and joy looking to the fulfillment of all things in that future which has already broken into our present.

Thus the Church must bear witness to Jesus Christ in the sight of the world religions, proclaiming, declaring and expounding his Gospel. She will do this without imposing herself; without condescendingly playing the part of the one who

always knows better and already enjoys possession of everything, as though she were mistress over the world's religions
and people; without misusing them as an object on which to
exercise her unspiritually spiritual power. She will do it in all
humility, modesty and unselfishness, in profound respect for
the freedom of every individual, every group, every community, every people. If she does it like this, not so as to dominate but to serve, not so as to overpower but to liberate, then
it is also permitted to her to do it boldly and decisively, un-
compromisingly and with genuine insistence, in all the richness and variety of the different articulations and charisms and
forms and structures which make up her ministry of witness.

Thus *all the members* of the Church should be witnesses,
not devoting themselves self-centeredly to ensuring the salvation of their own souls, understood in an individualistic way,
but being truly witnesses of the Gospel each according to the
charism given to him. All the various functions of the Church
should witness to Christ, arising out of his Gospel, and thus
not being simply esoteric ecclesiastical activities for their own
sake, but a service and witness in the world and among its
religions. This applies to the churches of the *homelands*:
today they have to stand more and more in existential confrontation, not only with the quasi-religions, but also, because
of the unification of mankind, with the real world religions.
All the Church's functions have got to be a service of witness
before the world; they must keep the world in view and, directly or indirectly, serve the work of *evangelization*, of witness to Christ's Gospel among those who are nearest at hand,
the merely nominal Christians. And most especially, of course,
it applies to the young churches which are called to witness
to the message of Christ in the midst of the world religions.
All the Church's functions have got to be a service of witness

to the world, directed toward the world religions, directly or indirectly serving the "mission," understood in the best sense of the word: the work of witnessing to the Gospel of Christ among the peoples of the world religions who stand so far off from the Church.

It is true that there are forms of the service of witness which by their very nature are directed inward rather than outward, toward the Church herself rather than toward the world. But however spiritual the preaching; however beautiful the liturgy; however well-organized the pastoral care; however thorough the instruction; however effective the charitable work; however profound the theology—what would be the good of it all if it were exclusively for the benefit of a church basking in her own self-sufficiency and living only for herself? If it were not also for the benefit of the world, for whose sake the Church is supposed to exist? Can a Christian or a church pray and offer praise, preach and teach and do their theology and their pastoral and charitable work without being mindful of their brothers in the real and quasi-religions of the world, their brothers who share with these Christians and this church a common origin, a common road, a common goal, a common Father and Redeemer? In everything that we do or leave un-done in the Church, the world outside the Church, the hu-man beings of the world religions and the quasi-religions, are present too, now attending to it, now ignoring it, now silent, now speaking, now protesting, now thanking. . . . The Church needs to be conscious of the fact that, if she wants to be the Church at all, she cannot exist other than as evangelizing and being witness in the sight of the world. Is there still any need today to spend words on pointing out that if this witness is to achieve its object in Asia and Africa it must not be preached and enacted in Western, Latin, Roman dress?

The Church must not forget for a single moment that
what she is doing really ought to be being done by all: that
the part of humanity which is in the world religions really
ought to believe in the Gospel of Christ too, that it too ought
to know about the grace of God and the justification, sanctification and vocation of the sinner; that it too should be offering thanks and praise, practicing the love of neighbor in daily
life, and awaiting the fulfillment of our redemption that is
still to come, the reign of God; for that which has been done
by God in Christ has not only been done for the Church but
for all, irrevocably. Hence the Church must not forget for a
single moment that she can and must do all this as representative for the people of the world religions who know nothing
of what has been done for them.

Thus the Church, in her manifold witness to the Gospel of
Christ, stands before God, the common Father of all, as the
representative of mankind in the world religions; while well
aware of the distance and alienation from God of the people
in the world religions, she does not address her appeal to them
in terms of this past alienation which has been brought to a
close in Christ, but in terms of the future which has been
opened in Christ. Not only because it would be pedagogically
unsound, but because it would be theologically false, the
Church will not address herself polemically to these peoples
as to antagonists and enemies: as though God had not already
declared in their favor, in Christ, and already had mercy on
them too; as though they were not already redeemed; as
though this did not mean that the whole of their paganism,
their remoteness and alienation, has already been overcome.
Man in the world religions is not to be approached in terms
of that unbelieving understanding and misunderstanding of
himself which God's grace has already overcome, but in terms

of a new, believing understanding of himself, which is his own future already breaking into his present. For

> We cannot truly call on God, the Father of all, if we refuse to treat in a brotherly way any man, created as he is in the image of God. Man's relation to God the Father and his relation to men his brothers are so linked together that Scripture says: "He who does not love does not know God" (1 John 4:8).
>
> No foundation therefore remains for any theory or practice that leads to discrimination between man and man or people and people, so far as their human dignity and the rights flowing from it are concerned.
>
> The Church reproves, as foreign to the mind of Christ, any discrimination against man or harassment of them because of their race, color, condition of life, or religion. On the contrary, following in the footsteps of the holy Apostles Peter and Paul, this sacred synod ardently implores the Christian faithful to "maintain good fellowship among the nations" (1 Peter 2:12), and if possible, to live for their part in peace with all men, so that they may truly be sons of the Father who is in heaven.*

What, then, is the Church's task among the world religions? The Church is not a privileged, exclusive club for those who have got salvation as opposed to those who have not got it. She is not the "exclusive community of those awaiting salvation" but "the historically visible vanguard, . . . the explicit embodiment, historically and socially constituted, of some-

* Second Vatican Council's *Declaration on the Relation of the Church to Non-Christian Religions*, 5.

thing which the Christian hopes is also given as a hidden reality outside the visibility of the church."* She is, as Israel was, the *pars pro toto*, the minority there to serve the majority, "the small number which represents the whole."† She is —to make use of an expression of the First Vatican Council— the *signum levatum in nationes* (Denziger, 1794), the sign of the last times lifted up among the nations of the world, the sign of the fulfillment of all things which is the work of God, and which is already visibly initiated in her.

So as the vanguard of humanity, as the sign to the peoples, the Church is the community of believers, who are witnesses of Christ, confessing him in word and deed. They believe and confess that which is already a reality for the people of the world religions too, even though they do not wish to acknowledge it. As this community of believers and witnesses confessing Christ in word and deed, the Church is a living invitation, a joyful challenge to the people of the world religions, calling on them to unite with her in faith and to witness with her to the great things which God the Lord has done not only for her but for all; to join in offering praise and thanks, in listening ever anew to the word of God, and celebrating ever again the banquet of love, in witnessing to Christ in daily life as people who love not only each other, but all others as well. The Church is this sign of invitation to the peoples so that from Christians *de jure* they may become Christians *de facto*; from Christians *in spe*, Christians *in re*; that from being Christians by designation and vocation they may become Christians by profession and witness.

As vanguard and sign to the peoples, the Church is thus the image—an imperfect and obscure image, yet still clear

* Rahner *op. cit.*, p. 156.
† Y. Congar, *Ausser der Kirche Kein Heil* (Essen, 1961), p. 21.

enough to be recognizable, in the power of the Spirit—of what has already been inaugurated but which we still await in its completed form, the eschatological, ultimate, universal Reign of God. In her whole existence, in all that she is and does during this interim period between the first Easter and the last she is there to be a prophetic proclamation, image and representation of that which is promised to us: the calling of *every* human being, of the *whole* of mankind, indeed the whole world, into the service of God, and thus into the *doxa*, the full revelation of the glory of God, when God, who is already in all things, will be all in all.

5 THE FREEDOM OF A POPE

Where the Spirit of the Lord is,
there is freedom.
                    2 Cor. 3, 17

The hardly to be wondered at, but yet somewhat exciting variations of opinion. . . . This
too corresponds to the plan of divine Providence, to set the truth in its right light and to
make plain before the whole world the holy
freedom of the children of God, which has its
place in the Church.   *John XXIII*

John XXIII was not what the world would call a great speaker or a great diplomat, a great linguist, a great jurist or a great scholar. In fact, with all his remarkable intuitive intelligence, he was not really what Church history would call a great theologian. And yet if I were asked and—without anticipating the verdict of history—were to answer, simply and spontaneously, the question, "Who is the greatest pope of this century?" I should unhesitatingly reply, "John XXIII." And if someone were to point out to me all the great things that John XXIII was not—but who would be interested since Pope John did just this himself in his coronation address?— then I would say that ultimately none of that matters when compared with the one thing in which he was great: *service*. And in this he has behind him the word of another, who puts his greatness beyond dispute: "If any one would be first, he must be last of all and servant of all."

And wasn't it this that made this pope so popular, indeed, so loved by countless millions both inside and outside the Catholic Church? This pope was not, like so many of his predecessors, wondered at, admired, or even feared. He was loved. Here was a man who, without any pretentiousness whatever, but in profound freedom simply did his job. He never considered himself as special; he disliked posed photographs in pious attitudes and made jokes about not being photogenic. And yet pictures of him were always attractive and often touching: this face without guile, humble, kind, lovable. John XXIII did not pretend to knowledge when he had none. He did not pretend that he wrote every official document ("I've read it!" he said once, with a chuckle, of his first encyclical). But whenever he spoke, his words, inspired by the Gospel, went straight to the heart. The Roman pomp which surrounded him, difficult to remove, he was totally indifferent to. He had little time for demonstrations of honor towards him. He did without the *sedia gestatoria* whenever he could and entered St. Peter's on foot. In order to avoid an ovation as he came into the basilica he had the Apostles' Creed sung. He personally introduced concelebration in St. Peter's. He loved to pray with the faithful in St. Peter's Square at midday from his window, but always withdrew immediately in order to avoid any ovation.

Evangelical Freedom

What makes a man great in the eyes of other men was of no concern to John XXIII; but what makes a man great—according to the Gospel—in the eyes of God, was important to him. And it was this specifically evangelical quality which distinguished him from his great predecessors. Not only was he strictly opposed to all family politics and all nepotism. Not only did he, as the Bishop of Rome, concern himself in a new —or rather old—way about his own flock and his own clergy, visiting individual parishes in the suburbs himself. No, the chief thing was that, without making any fuss about it, he reminded us of old evangelical truths which, in Rome of all places, had been strangely forgotten. Who of his great predecessors had ever, as Pope, personally visited the poor, comforted the sick in hospitals, sought out priests who had suffered a breakdown? Who had gone to the Roman state prison and, in a place which would severely test the greatest speakers, found the right words to say? Simply, he told the prisoners and criminals, who never dreamed of such a visit, that prisons had always affected him profoundly since his boyhood, because his own uncle had gone to jail for poaching. The *Osservatore Romano*, which often suppressed the best thing in the Pope's speeches, replaced the word "uncle" with "relation"—apparently more in keeping with the dignity of the Pope. . . .

Pope John never tried to appear an extraordinary man, or a saint in his own lifetime. If anyone had called him that he would certainly have laughed. He never stood on his dignity. During the Council he received a great national conference of bishops for which he had prepared an address in French, but the speech of greeting to him was in Latin. He therefore felt compelled to give his address in Latin also, but his translation from French to Latin was not altogether successful. He apologized, saying that he had not made any speeches in Latin since the time he taught church history at a seminary. Leaving the room he said to the bishops, "Oggi abbiamo fatto una brutta figura!" ("Today we cut a poor figure!") And after *Veterum Sapientia* (the constitution in favor of church Latin, which a few Roman prelates had forced out of him), he said, "But I didn't write it myself!" So he was never too solemn about himself. As he once told a bishop, if he could not sleep for worry he would let "the Pope" say, "Angelo, don't take yourself so seriously!"

All men of good will always felt with this man that he did not want to be there for himself, but only for others. He did not want to force people, he wanted to convince through love. He did not want to instruct from on high; he wanted, from a deep understanding of the achievements and the needs of the modern world, to help as a brother. That could be heard in everything he said and particularly in his last encyclical *Pacem in Terris*, which, with its message of peace and justice, religious freedom, human rights and the brotherhood of all men, echoed round the world. John XXIII thus made the office of Peter within the Church, often elevated to an institution between heaven and earth, more human again and more lovable. Or rather, he tried to make the office of Peter, based on the Gospels, evangelical in a new way, according to the demands of the Gospel. That is why Pope John was so popular with the Evangelical Church. That is why he was a great pope. That is why he was free indeed.

Friendly to the Communists?

In the fundamental area of doctrine and ethics John XXIII never made the slightest concession to Communism. On the contrary, he always demanded, in opposition to totalitarianism, respect for the dignity, the freedom, and the rights of the individual in state and society. But he was profoundly convinced that it is not sufficient to be simply "against" something. He saw the *positive* task of being responsible for *all* Christians and for *all* men—including those behind the Iron Curtain, whom we always praise in theory, but in practice are largely written off. Pope John was never ready to write them off.

The invitation of the spiritual representatives of the Russian Orthodox Church was a courageous decision. John XXIII, for a long time Apostolic Delegate in countries of the Orthodox persuasion, knew how important the attitude of the Russian Orthodox Church to the Council and its endeavors would be for the attitude of all the Orthodox churches. He knew that by far the largest part of the Eastern church—many, many millions—live within the sphere of Russian political influence. He wanted to help these millions of suffering Christians, Catholic and non-Catholic. Help and service were here, as always, uppermost in his mind, not strategy and politics. That is why he invited representatives of these Christians. It was certainly reasons of political opportunism which made the Soviet Government agree to the representatives attending the Council. For the Russian Orthodox Church itself, however, it was of the greatest importance to make contact for the first time in long decades with the Catholic Church at its heart, to listen, to observe, and to reply. Those who spoke to the Russian observers at the Council know with what dignity these two priests, one of whom has since been made a bishop, fulfilled their task, and how totally unpolitical they considered it to be. For them it was ecclesiastical and pastoral, and they were delighted with this new contact with the Catholic Church, whose representatives were in Rome from every continent. They were grateful that the Pope had not forgotten the millions of Orthodox Christians behind the Iron Curtain. The taking up of certain personal and diplomatic contacts with political representatives of the East had the same unpolitical, pastoral character. There was no question of intellectual capitulation to Communism or of dismissing the witness of Christians who have suffered for their faith in many ways and continue to do so. On the contrary, it was a matter of helping these suffering Christians in their need, of alleviating their situation, of assisting the Church in these countries as much as possible, both its faithful and its pastors —with no reference to questions of prestige and of day-to-day politics.

The Pope's invitation to the Russian Orthodox observers and the consequent respect for their feelings prevented the Council from being misused for the purposes of a purely negative anti-Communism, widespread in Italy, which is strong in words and weak in deeds. One of the first official acts of the newly-elected pope was to improve the wages and the social standing of the Vatican employees. In practice and in theory he pursued social reforms. Was it surprising that this man, who felt for the poor of this country of vast class differences, with all his aversion for the Communist system, should have little time for the anti-Communism of those who fight Communism with manifestoes and programs alone, but who avoid social reforms wherever they can, support appalling corruption in the State administration, tolerate on the one hand unimaginable luxury, and on the other equally unimaginable misery, but who, when it comes to elections and other political action, are always glad to enlist the aid of the Church, its preaching and its pastoral work, for their not particularly Christian purposes?

In some circles Pope John has been blamed for the increase of the Communist vote in the Italian elections. Nothing is more unjust. But if one wishes to defend Pope John against this charge it will be necessary to bring out into the open some facts which may possibly shock. The responsibility for the increase in the Communist vote—apart from political factors—rests largely with the failure of the Italian Church to deal with the problems of the moment. To put it bluntly, how long has it, instead of preaching the gospel, preferred to become involved in politics? Instead of realizing the gospel, preferred to distribute pamphlets and collect votes? But how can a Church be equipped for a positive confrontation with Communism when its masses suffer from appalling religious ignorance, from superstition and poverty of belief (so often the result of bad, moralizing or sentimental sermons and superficial instruction which bears little relation to life); when its clergy—to the regret of many good Italian priests—are educated within a seminary system as insulated from the world as possible; when its theology—to the regret of many gifted Italian theologians—because of a fundamental lack of intellectual freedom, has hardly produced one work of international importance; when its services—to the regret of many outstanding Catholic laymen—are unable to generate any sense of Christian community; when it has largely lost contact with the intellectuals and with the workers? This is the problem of Communism in Italy, as far as it involves the Church—in spite of all the fine and heroic work that individual laymen and priests do, often more than in our own countries. And it was this that John XXIII sought to remedy: by the universal renewal of the Church. He could not fail to see that decrees of excommunication had achieved nothing in Italy, but that the number of Communist votes was rising slowly but constantly even before his pontificate. John XXIII wanted, with the help of the Ecumenical Council, the positive renewal of the Church and of religious life especially within the Italian Church and—precisely in order to combat anticlericalism—a little more distance between the Church and internal Italian party politics. Didn't this involve taking certain risks? Better

now than later! It was late enough, as it was. John XXIII,
who saw further than his critics, wanted, through selfless service, to help remedy this situation.

Open to All Christians and to the World

John XXIII will go down in church history as the pope
who was able, as it were, overnight to bring the Church out
of its reserve towards the ecumenical movement and make it
ecumenically active. Of course there had been ecumenical
endeavors before in the Catholic Church. But they involved
only a tiny advanced guard of theologians and laymen. Pope
John made the reunion of separated Christians a concern of
the whole Church and particularly of its center. Of course he
was not the first to "open wide his arms"—as one used to say
in Rome—towards other Christians. But it was generally an
invitation to return, and nothing more. John XXIII was the
first to show that opening one's arms was not enough, but that
one also had to busy one's hands, in order to do one's own
share of the work on the Catholic side to smooth the way
towards reunion.

Preparation for reunion with separated Christians through
the renewal of the Catholic Church itself! This was the tremendous program he set the Second Vatican Council, this
Council, which is essentially *his* Council. No one forced him
to do it, no one advised him to do it. It was his decision and
his program. It was not as a great church strategist that he
set in motion this epoch-making event. Church politics in the
usual sense of the word were foreign to him. It was not even
as a great theologian that he thought out this project full of
dangers and of unforeseen possibilities, considered its dogmatic and historical basis, and worked out its theoretical and

practical consequences. "Are you a theologian?" he asked a well-known Anglican minister. "No." "*Tant mieux*—neither am I!"

John XXIII conceived the idea of the Council out of the simple, childlike faith of a believing Christian convinced that with God's help something serious had to be done about the tragic divisions of the Church. He summoned this Council as a man of God who did not let himself be frightened by the risks of such an undertaking, but was always sustained by a holy optimism which was nothing other than unconquerable, realistic Christian hope. He knew the difficulties in the way of the idea of the Council in his immediate vicinity. But "Il concilio si deve fare malgrado la Curia"—"The Council must be held in spite of the Curia," he once said to some priests from his Bergamasque home, who were amazed that not everyone in Rome thought like the Pope.

He proceeded with caution and with great astuteness. He was helped by a quite unsentimental Christian love, which guided him in his everyday dealings. Hence his aversion for blind condemnations, thoughtless anathematizations and excommunications, against unjust inquisitional practices. He never offended anyone. He often achieved what he wanted inconspicuously and by apparently roundabout methods: "Papa Giovanni, like the water, always gets what he's after," one of his friends told me. For a while he permitted his aides to pass over in silence the ecumenical purpose of the Council. "But I'll be bringing it in again," he said to a visitor who complained about it. And he founded the Secretariat for Promoting Christian Unity. An important factor in the success of the Council hitherto has been that the head of this Secretariat, Cardinal Bea, always had, even in the most difficult undertakings, the Pope's full confidence.

John XXIII was a pragmatist who thought intuitively. And this was an advantage to the Council and to its ecumenical endeavors. This pope had no time for that doctrinalism which —because of its Pharisaism, its intolerance, and its lack of understanding for the genuine concerns of others—is the greatest and most dangerous enemy of the Council and of all ecumenical activity. That is why he told the theological preparatory commission not to prepare any formal new dogmas. Pope John was convinced that humanity is not best helped in its present situation by the repetition or definition of old truths, but by a proclamation of the Gospel appropriate to our own day, which will make use of new modes of expression and be able to distinguish between the substance and the trappings of the old teaching. He stated that with great emphasis to the Council in his opening address, and it had great influence on the course of the Council's deliberations. John XXIII had no ambition to go down in history as a pope who, without being challenged by heresy, defined a new dogma. "I am not infallible," he once remarked in a conversation with Greek seminarians. When they looked at him in surprise, he said with a smile, "No, I'm not infallible. The Pope is infallible only when he speaks *ex cathedra*. But I will never speak *ex cathedra*." He never spoke *ex cathedra*.

In his ecumenical labors Pope John never bothered about questions of prestige, which largely prevent, or render purely formal in themselves, natural contacts and meetings between Christians (e.g., between Catholic and Lutheran bishops). The naturalness and warmth with which he received his non-Catholic visitors were often praised by them. During the Council he said to two brothers from the Protestant community of Taizé, "Oh, you've dressed in white!" "Normally we dress in ordinary clothes," replied the brothers, "but we put

on this white robe for services." "Oh, vous savez," laughed
John, "je ne suis pas jaloux!"—"I'm not jealous!" He possessed
great ecumenical tact and accepted in natural friendliness,
against all the reservations of protocol and of church diplo-
macy which his advisers made, the gifts of Eastern orthodox
dignitaries and gave them presents in return. A new sense of
Christian brotherhood filled the heart of this bishop, who
always wanted to be a bishop among bishops and who so often
preferred not to bless the people alone, but only with his
brother bishops. This new sense of Christian brotherhood
prevented him from letting the Council meet without the
representatives of the other Christian communities. When he
received them in the Vatican during the Council he did not
want to sit on the papal throne. He asked for a chair and sat
simply with them: "For you I am not Peter's successor!"

Let no one say that these things are trifles. They reveal a
whole attitude. They succeeded in changing the whole climate.
During the five years of his pontificate the ecumenical situation improved more than in fifty years, indeed, almost more
than in five hundred years. Is it surprising that all men of
good will—to whom he dedicated his last encyclical, *Pacem in
Terris*—are grateful to him, and that not only Christians, but
also Jews, whom he was particularly fond of, prayed for his
life? All these men realized that here was a man who only
wanted to serve: the Church, Christendom, the world, all men.
Right up to his painful death, about which he had known for
a long time, he endured in this service without drawing any
attention to himself whatsoever.

The Catholic Church, after John XXIII, can never be the
same again. A new era of church history started with him, an
era of new freedom, of new life, of new hope. His last wish
on his death-bed was that the Council might continue and

bring forth abundantly. Of course there will be fresh opposition and fresh difficulties in the way of his program. But the Catholic Church will continue along the road that John XXIII has opened up. His program—the renewal of the Church service to the world, reunion with separated Christians—has not only a pope, but the Lord of the Church himself behind it.

John XXIII is less forgotten today than ever. His greatness increases as we become more separated from him in time. As recently as the Spring of 1965, many hundreds of learned men and statesmen gathered together in New York from every continent and from the most diverse political and religious views for the express purpose of considering and discussing Pope John's encyclical, "Pacem in Terris." John XXIII was open to the world, open to the world's needs and hopes. And so the world, in turn, opened itself to him.

The world experienced in John XXIII the freedom of a Pope. Who does not find this particularly astounding in an institution next to which the old dynasties with their ancient traditions, even the states of old Europe with their long histories, must all be called young? It had not at all been expected. On the contrary, the world had become accustomed to looking upon the Pope as "the prisoner of the Vatican."

And then came one who, precisely as Pope, practiced the naturalness of the glorious freedom of God's children: *la santa libertà degli figli di Dio*, as he himself used to call it. This man was, to a staggering degree, free *from* empty ceremony and courtly formality, free *from* forced protocol and considerations of prestige, free *from* palace intriguing and diplomatic machinations, free *from* personal resentment and historical prejudices and complexes, free *from* outdated traditions and sterile conventions, free *from* narrow nationalisms and Roman provincialism, free *from* scholastic doctrinalism and intolerant inquisitionalism, free *from* overrating Canon Law and Church definitions, free *from* all forms of juridism and triumphalism, free *from* false dignity and haughty condescending, free *from* clerical arrogance and hierarchical greed for power.

And to a likewise staggering degree, he was free *to* think and act without inhibitions, free *to* take daring steps and *to* embrace the unfamiliar and the new, free *to* assume necessary risks and *to* live with unshakable trust, free *to* lend assistance selflessly and with enthusiasm, free *to* bring a fresh and uncomplicated spirit to the original Gospel of Jesus Christ, free *to* engage in a new encounter between Catholics and Non-Catholics, between Christians and Non-Christians, free and open *to* a new understanding of the modern world, free and open *to* men, *to* all mankind.

What is the secret of the great freedom of this Pope, indeed the secret of all genuine freedom? The secret is Love. It is in Love that the Spirit of God himself is free to work. God himself is both the Love that is free and the freedom that loves. *Ama—et fac quod vis*, says Augustine: Love—and do what you will.